How Long is Long Ago?

BACK TO THE FUTURE

Paul H. Strege

*It was so good,
Darar, to have
you join our family!*

Paul

Chipmunk Chapel Books
St. Louis, MO

BY THE SAME AUTHOR

How Small is Small?
How Far is Far?
How Free is Free?
How Near is Near?
©*2000, 2002, 2004, 2007*

How Long is Long Ago?
Back to the Future

Published by Chipmunk Chapel Books
8343 Lonkar Drive, St. Louis, MO 63123-3449

ISBN-10: 0-9705121-8-X

ISBN-13: 978-0-9705121-8-5

Printed by:

Independent Publishing Corporation

St. Louis, Missouri

Email author at:

phstrege@att.net

Cover photos: Arthur and Paul Strege, 1928; Paul & Vercile Strege and Paul & Alleen Heerboth, Japan, 1949.

ACKNOWLEDGEMENTS

The compilation of this book has been a labor of love involving numerous people in many places. Some were relatively "passive" as subjects of many of the stories recorded and retold in far-flung parts of the U.S., Japan and even Africa. Special thanks go to the contributors of creative ideas like Paul Heerboth in suggesting the title for the book and son John who envisioned the concept for the cover, which was created with the talents of granddaughter, Faith and her husband, Lonnie Colson. Lietta Haenel spent many hours reading the manuscripts and making helpful suggestions for improvement. All 18 grandchildren deserve recognition for contributing stories that constitute one whole section of the book. Sons Mark and John provided the photos from Japan, and son Tim deserves special recognition for formatting the book for the printer. I consider all of them special gifts of God, Whom I thank for bringing all components together to produce "How Long is Long Ago?"

.

FOREWORD

He wasn't sure they were there — enough stories, that is, to fill Book Five. But once again, Paul Strege is delighting us with stories spanning 85 years. Stories of the not-so-long ago return visit in 2008 to Japan to long ago growing up in Ludell, Kansas.

And what finer tribute to a beloved grandmother and grandfather than memories and stories from all eighteen grandchildren.

Book Five is unique in that pictures accompany the three sections.

What is apparent throughout this book are the blessings and miracles of our Lord Jesus Christ. He has sustained and guided the Strege Family these many years as recounted herein. It is my prayer that God will continue to bless them and all who read this book.

Lietta Haenel

CONTENTS

PREFACE

Three Parts

Julius Caesar began a history of the Roman Empire with the words (in Latin): "Gaul (modern France) is divided into three parts."

The same is true of this book—it is divided into three parts.

The first part is a pictorially illustrated report of an exciting trip by four of the six Strege children and me, their father, in 2008, back to Japan, where they lived their childhood years.

The second part is written by a younger generation—my 18 grandchildren—with reflections on their experiences of the past and hopes as they look to the future. **It is to those 18 grandchildren that this book is dedicated.**

The third part looks back to the longer past in the generation of my growing up and beyond, including pictorial illustrations.

The title and subtitle of the book are meant to reflect some of the time element covered by the stories remembered and recorded, and were suggested by Paul Heerboth, my lifelong friend and mentor. The title, "How Long is Long Ago?" is embellished by the subtitle mirroring the generational nature of the family history: "Back to the Future!"

Hopefully the readers will experience some of the drama and excitement of the writers!

The Author

PART 1   Japan -- Here We Come!

Can You Go Back?

"Dad, you can stay here if you want, but we're going back to Japan!"

It was the summer of 1966, and our family was in St. Louis on a one-year home leave from mission work in Japan. All six Strege children had been born while we lived in Japan, considered it home, and were anticipating returning to Japan again in a few months. But the Mission Board under which I served made some dramatic changes in structure and announced that my office would be transferred from Tokyo to St. Louis, effective immediately. That meant the family would not be moving to Tokyo—and elicited the statement above by the four older children who had attended school in Japan.

Of course, they mistakenly made the assumption that I "wanted to" move the office from Japan to St. Louis, not necessarily true. But there were no other options, and everyone involved made the adjustment to reality.

However, the children never forgot their determination to go back, and 42 years later, in June 2008, occasioned by the 50th anniversary of the Hokkaido International School (HIS), which we had a part in organizing in 1958—and which they attended until 1965—went back! And they took me along!

HIS, organized by several mission group representatives, opened as a one-room school in 1958 with eight children, two of them from the Strege family. By 2008 it had not only expanded to grades K-12, but also had graduated 1000 students from the 12th grade. With Japanese government assistance, it is on its third campus with facilities to handle an enrollment of 300 students, some of them living in a school-owned dormitory.

Our campus visit was a highlight of the two weeks we spent in Japan and demonstrated that "you can go back," even though 42 years later!

Hokkaido International School in June 2008

Unbelievable

John was coordinating plans for the trip back to Japan for two weeks in June 2008. There were seven of us signed on: daughter Ruth and her husband, Keith, daughter Mary and her daughter, Joy, sons John, Mark and I. I suggested to John that he e-mail our itinerary to a long-time friend, Japanese Pastor Kazuteru Matsukawa, for suggestions about hotels he would recommend for our overnight accommodations. He responded that he would not only recommend, but also book us into hotels in Tokyo, Yokohama, Kyoto and Sapporo. Further, he suggested we purchase rail-passes to accommodate our travel needs.

However, he shared no information about the hotel costs. After waiting a number of weeks, John specifically asked him for some figures to help us in our financial planning. His response was, "About the money, don't worry, I will pay it!" Unbelievable! Two weeks of hotel charges for seven persons!!

This came about after many decades of connections between the Matsukawa and Strege families. When Kazuteru was a university student in Hokkaido in the late 1950s I was able to arrange for a little "arbeit"—a German term used for part-time

11

compensated work—by signing him on to help in the Lutheran Hour Bible Correspondence Course office in Sapporo. After he was married he and his wife lived in our home in Sapporo during our family's three-month home leave in the U.S. They moved to Tokyo when he enrolled in the seminary. As their three children were born he and his wife requested Vercile and me to serve as their baptismal sponsors. A number of times in the 70s, 80s and 90s when our family lived in St. Louis he spent overnights in our home enroute to or from church related or International Rotary Club meetings in the U.S., Europe and elsewhere. He also hosted us for overnight stays in Tokyo when Vercile and I were there in 1995 and 1998. So there have been long time family-to-family relations.

Unbelievable, nevertheless! And most gratefully accepted!

Rev. Matsukawa with Ruth, Paul and Mary

Will We Make It?

It was a rather tight schedule. Mark and I would fly from St. Louis to Chicago to join the other five in our family group to board the flight to Tokyo. There was only a one-hour layover scheduled at O'Hare to make the connection.

12

We checked our bags and cleared security bright and early on the morning of June 19, only to be confronted with one announcement after another that our flight from St. Louis would be delayed. We contacted the five in Chicago by cell-phone and nervousness set in as to whether we would make the connection or not. Along the way we learned that there were two or three additional persons on our flight from St. Louis also planning to make connection with the flight to Tokyo

Paul and Mark, a long wait!

When we finally landed at O'Hare, instead of pulling up to a gate on the concourse our plane stopped on the ground level apron, the stairs were lowered and we were ushered off the plane and hurried up a wooden inclined walk-way, a stairway and down long hallways to suddenly arrive at the front entry door of the jumbo jet filled with hundreds of passengers ready to take off for Tokyo. United Airlines had held up the plane for us to board! Wouldn't you know—of course—our seats were in the rear section, so we had another long walk through the narrow aisle to be greeted, finally, by our five family members with warm shouts of welcome! There was hardly time to be seated before we were taxiing to the runway for takeoff!!

Having done appreciable air travel over a lifetime, there was a lagging concern in my mind during the thirteen-hour flight to Tokyo as to whether there was any way that our checked bags could be on the plane with us. But—miracle of miracles—when we disembarked at Tokyo's Narita airport, our bags had also arrived!

13

So Tired

Miles or kilometers—we covered a lot of them our first day in Japan! From the hotel to the train station where we boarded the train to the Kudan-shita station, and from there to the famous Yasukuni Shinto Shrine, where the souls of the dead of Japan's wars—including WWII—are enshrined. The distance from the huge Torii Gate at the entrance to the Shrine itself is several city blocks long. From there John had planned our walk skirting Meiji Park and across a bridge over the mote that surrounds the grounds of the Imperial Palace. That "scotched" my long held impression that the public was not permitted in the Palace grounds since they include the home of the Emperor and his family. Beautiful large hydrangea bushes were in full bloom along the edge of spacious lawns interspersed with ancient stone monuments and walls. When we finally crossed the mote again at another entrance/exit of the Imperial Palace we faced the challenge of crossing one of Tokyo's busiest streets. And we were hungry and thirsty!

Yasukuni Shrine

Several more blocks of walking brought us to the large Marunouchi Building, which I remembered from the time we lived in Japan in the 1950's. It was now converted into a "restaurant haven" (my title)! Entering a door, we were at the

14

foot of an escalator to the second floor, which we discovered housed one restaurant after another all around the building. The same was true when we took escalators to the third and fourth floors—all the way to the seventh floor. Choices—choices—choices! How could we decide which of the fancy—and expensive looking specialized menu restaurants—to enter for lunch?—Until off in one corner of the fourth floor we saw one with a large neon sign above the door: "SO TIRED." That was the invitation we needed—it looked to us like "S-O-O-O-O-O TIRED!" and we rested our weary bones and enjoyed an affordable repast!

The Ginza

The street named "Ginza" is traditionally known as the center of the downtown shopping district of Tokyo, so tourists never miss visiting it. Nor did we! But to our surprise, at the main shopping intersection, we noted the cross street closed off to vehicular traffic for several blocks and was like an outdoor walking mall. Conveniently spaced resting-benches had been placed in the center of the street with roofs for protection from the sun and any rain that might fall. An innocuous street sweeper with broom and dustpan picked up any possible debris shoppers may have dropped.

As the rest of the shoppers in the family walked the street Mark and I sat down to rest on one of the benches. In a few minutes a young lady joined us in the empty space next to me. She was, of course, quite shocked when I greeted her in Japanese, and told us that she was a dress designer for the large department store we were facing, to which she returned after what was apparently a rest period for her.

The experience was evidence to us that in the rushing seemingly constant activity of the Japanese, government leaders thoughtfully arranged for a quiet spot in the center of the busy city to grab a few minutes of rest.

Ruth, Paul, and John on the Ginza.

Masked Invaders

After a busy and tiring first day of hiking in Tokyo and "dinner" in a street-side restaurant near the subway station, we walked back to our hotel and gathered in one of our rooms to review the day. In short order the cold drinks—including a few beers—for the seven of us ran out and granddaughter Joy volunteered to go to a nearby shop we had passed along the street to pick up a few replacements for us.

Not too much later the door suddenly opened and two large masked men rushed in shouting and making a big ruckus! It didn't take long for us to recognize them as two grandsons, Andrew from Los Angeles and Chris from Chicago, who had

16

secretly arranged to join us as a surprise—and a surprise it was, even to their parents in the room!!!

Without ever breathing a word to any of us for months, Joy had informed her brother, Chris, and cousin, Andrew, of our plans, itinerary and all, including which hotel we would be staying at, and they booked themselves into the same hotel and flew over the Pacific to be a part of our entourage for a week! So our "family" of seven suddenly became nine.

Grandsons Chris Petry and Andrew Forni as they unexpectedly appeared at our hotel room door in Tokyo.

And Then We Were Ten

Sunday morning, and plans were to attend Roppongi Church, traveling by subway and foot. As we were gathering in the hotel lobby, there was a familiar stranger standing nearby. Who was he? It was cleared up for me when one of my children told me he was Daran Janecek from Paducah, Kentucky. Then it hit me! Daran is a member of St. Matthew Lutheran Church in Paducah, where my daughter, Lois, and family are members. I had met him there several months earlier at Easter and learned from him that a couple times a year he travels to China on business for his company. What I didn't know is that he requested—and received—information from Lois about details of her siblings and my trip to Japan, including dates and hotel reservations.

17

So Daran scheduled his next trip to China to include Saturday night in our hotel in Tokyo on his return trip home so he could attend church in Tokyo with us. And so we were ten of us walking the streets early Sunday morning to the subway and Roppongi Lutheran Church!

Several years earlier Roppongi Church had been built on land owned by the Japan Lutheran Church on which one of the first post-WWII Lutheran churches was established in 1948—housed in a rehabbed U.S. Army barracks building. Fifty some years later the land was made available to the Mori Development Company as the site for erection of a 54 story high-rise with the condition that Mr. Mori would build Lutheran Church facilities at the lower two-story level of the "Mori Towers." So as we left the Roppongi subway station we thought we were in exceptional good luck when in the distance ahead on the street we started to walk we saw two towering buildings with the words "MORI TOWERS" at the top. When we arrived we found they were office buildings, closed on Sunday, and it took some sleuthing around and rides in two taxis to handle a group of ten, to find that there are more than two Mori Towers, and we arrived at the correct one about 15 minutes before church began!

Ten visitors at Roppongi Church with Dr. Y. Tadokoro (front center), retired first president of the Japan Lutheran Church.

18

A fitting sequel to the story is that six months later, on Christmas Eve, I was privileged to preach at St. Matthew's in Paducah and make reference to our worshipping in Tokyo and to Christmas celebrations in Japan, and sensed the palpability of the connection between this congregation and God's mission in Japan because of the visit there of one of their own!

59 Years Later

In 1949 a number of guests celebrated my 25th birthday in the Danker home a few days after Vercile and I arrived in Tokyo. Fifty-nine years later I worshipped with members of my family as guests in the new Roppongi Lutheran Church on the same Azabu site. What a change!

25th birthday celebration Aug. 5, 1949. (Photo by R. Meyer)

The Roppongi Church is a merger of two of the earliest post-WWII Lutheran churches in Azabu and Meguro areas of Tokyo. It was exciting to be part of the congregational worshippers ranging in age from senior citizens to children. After the liturgical worship service, we were invited to a reception arranged especially for the "Strege family" of ten. What a joyous occasion as a large group—including friends from long ago whom I was privileged to baptize and/or work with 50 years earlier—provided a Japanese potluck dinner!

19

Roppongi reception June 22, 2008

Some of the "long-ago friends" came an hour or more by train, and it was 10 years since I had last met them. Two sisters even handed me an envelope with a gift to take back to the U.S. for International Partners in Mission, which I had co-founded 35 years ago.—a testimony to the fact that God's Mission is, indeed, global!

Long-time church leaders gather at reception.

1910 Cross Crosses the Pacific in 2008

"The Cross—Still in Mission" was highlighted on page 168 of the book, "How Free is Free?" in 2004. "Born" in 1910 as the altar cross (crucifix) at a new Immanuel Lutheran Church in Ludell, Kansas, where I was born and baptized in 1924, it "found" a new home in 1995 in Joliet, Illinois, where my son-in-law, Keith Forni, founded a new Hispanic "Santa Cruz" (Holy Cross) Lutheran Church. When Santa Cruz moved into larger church quarters, the cross moved to a new Hispanic mission in DeKalb, Illinois, in 2004. No longer needed there, since June 2008 it has a new home in Japan!

As the "Strege family" was preparing to travel to Japan after a 42-year hiatus we were faced with the happy challenge of taking a gift to our host, Pastor Kazuteru Matsukawa in Ofuna, south of Yokohama. Pastor Keith (daughter Ruth's husband) was traveling with us, and since the cross was "on vacation" from serving several churches and missions in the U. S., we could think of no more appropriate new home for it than one in connection with the ministry of Pastor Matuskawa in a father/son pastorate with his son, Kazuyoshi, in Japan. At a reception our third night in Japan, hosted by the Matsukawa family, we formally presented to them the 98 year old cross, which had just crossed the Pacific.

After we returned home, we received word from Pastor Matsukawa that it now stands on the altar of the "chapel" at one of the four Christian pre-school/kindergartens he and his son supervise, which have a combination of 500 children and 120 teachers. So the "traveling cross" has a new mission, serving during daily devotions among hundreds of children from both Christian and non-Christian homes.

What a journey the cross has had in ministries on both sides of the globe!

Pajama Day

Toward the end of the "school year" at the pre-school in St. Louis where I have read stories to the three to five-year-olds the past eight years, I have included reading of Dr. Seuss' "Sleep Book." Part of the "fun" of doing it was that the children all came to pre-school that day in their pajamas and lay down on the floor for their daily rest period at the end of the story. I even wore mine one year!

While visiting one of the oldest and largest Lutheran pre-schools in Totsuka, Japan, in 2008, I found out that every day was "pajama day" for them. After lunch eaten in several different classrooms, all of the children gathered in a large "tatami" (straw-mat) floored room, carrying small tote bags. Each of about 100 children knew where his or her assigned tatami area of the floor was, went there, pulled a pajama out of the tote bag and changed into it in the "privacy" of their own spots in the room.

Children eat lunch before "pajama rest time"

This is not too different from a customary practice in Japanese homes, many of them so small traditionally that the daytime living rooms became nighttime bedrooms with family members sleeping on "futon" (sleeping mats) on the tatami floor. After all of them had folded and placed their day-time outer clothing neatly in their tote bags, the lights went out and it was "rest time" for all the children.

We didn't stay long enough to see them back into their day-time clothes, but it seemed not only a practical, but also instructive, exercise for the children in neatly dressing and undressing for sleeping in their homes.

One of numerous "geta-bakko" (shoe boxes) at school entrances

Daibutsu

1252 A.D. That's over 750 years ago. It's when the colossal bronze Daibutsu—statue of Buddha—was completed in Kamakura, Japan. Historically it was in the Kamakura period of Japanese development, after the seat of government had been moved from the Nara and Kyoto areas of central Japan to the area south of modern day Tokyo and Yokohama. It was an engineering marvel, cast somehow in sections and "welded" together to make a hollow likeness of Buddha towering some 40 feet above ground level.

The Daibutsu was on our schedule to visit on day #3 in Japan, and didn't seem to have aged at all since the time Vercile and I had seen it 60 years earlier! Not only the Buddha itself, but also the temples and gardens around the Buddha were impressive as we walked along mountainside pathways smothered in large blooming hydrangea, looking out beyond the harbor to the sea and a peninsula beyond. A memorable experience!

John at the Daibutsu

A Full Day

It was a full day! We "traveled" by train, bus, automobile and a lot of shoe-leather!

We started at Pastor Matsukawa's Ofuna Lutheran Church and "Hoikuen" (pre-school), then to the Totsuka pre-school of 100+ children, and after lunch (the same menu as the kids) to the Daibutsu at Kamakura, including hiking the mountain side and "crawling" through a tunnel/cave on the grounds and, finally, to a formal reception in Kanagawa at the southern border of Yokohama. As we approached the doorway to the entrance, there was a large sign indicating this was the location of a special reception for the Strege family.

24

Strege Family Reception, 2nd floor

We didn't have time to change clothes, so there I was in a well-sweated checkered sport shirt entering a room of people dressed in formal attire, including two men in black top hats. But all that is forgotten as long ago friends meet again and exchange greetings!

We were seated at four long tables to enjoy a 10 to 12 course meal (I lost count along the way). In addition to the nine members of the Strege family, guests included several past-presidents of the church denomination, pastors and their wives, president of the 100+ member Tokyo/Yokohama area church women's organization and her husband, as well as several guests from the Philippines and Germany serving with the church in Japan.

Mrs. Kato, president of Women's Organization

At "introduction" time, Pastor Kashiki reminisced about my having baptized him and his wife (on separate occasions) in

25

Asahigawa, Hokkaido, over 50 years earlier, and characterized my ministry with the phrase, "You told us who Jesus is." What an honor! Can the Christian witness be stated any more simply?

Retired Pastor & Mrs. Kashiki

Later in the evening one of the young ladies from the Philippines told me about being in a village that I remember, also, having visited, decades ago, and reported that is where she learned "who Jesus is." It was striking to hear the same phrase used in references related to becoming Christian in different Asian countries!

The whole group (all event photos by Seiji Kato)

Luggage Parade

It must have been quite a sight for the local residents—a parade of seven Americans pulling their wheeled luggage along the

26

streets in Japan, and even into railway and subway stations! Can't they afford a taxi or two?

But that's what was happening! Obviously tourists—four men and three women! At times they even stopped at street corners, seemingly not sure which way to go.— Adding to the challenge were the sirens and whistles accompanying change of traffic lights at city intersections, apparently an aid for the blind!

For several days there were nine Americans, after two grandsons joined the original seven. At least on those days the younger men picked up the "burden" of the oldest white-haired geezer by pulling his bag!

Actually, there were good results for all of us, whether we were perceived as a bit foolish or not. – Example: None of us gained weight because of lack of exercise!

Beware: "Class" Distinctions!

It's helpful to know about the railway class system and how it works in Japan. We "learned" the hard way.

When boarding trains in Tokyo, all passengers on the station platform line up according to sections marked on the platform floor to accommodate walking directly into open doors after the trains stop. There's no time for dilly-dallying, because the doors open for only "a minute" or so, and the lines are usually long. One day, preparing to embark, each of us in our family group was pulling one or two "wheeled" baggage pieces.

Surprise! The lines where we were standing to board were very short, so we had no trouble getting onto the train. And what luxury awaited us! Hardly any crowd of passengers, and it was easy to negotiate the few steps separating passengers on two levels of the car, plus there was room for our bags!

Surprise #2! The train barely started moving when a young lady "conductress" entered the car and announced that this car was for a special reserved seat class, which our tickets didn't accommodate. So we would need to move to the next car for "regular" passengers—an almost impossible challenge! Nine persons with some 12 pieces of luggage, most of them rather large, transferring while on a moving train to another car that was already crowded full of people, many even standing in the aisle!!

It's a long story without a short ending, as we pushed and pulled and lifted—and continued to be urged by the conductress to keep moving. Pieces of luggage piled one on top of another, with us between them like sardines! During that "emergency" another one developed as a Japanese woman passenger needed to cross the aisle to get from her seat to the small restroom on the other side because she was on the verge of vomiting!

Miraculously, she made it—and all of us survived until we reached our destination!

28

We didn't make the same mistake again!

Welcome aboard!

How's the air up there, Keith & John?

Bicycles Galore!

Be careful traversing the sidewalks in the cities of Japan because you are competing with bicycle riders! And they are welcomed there! In fact, the usual generously wide sidewalks are marked into separate "lanes" for walkers and bike riders.

The whole arrangement is an excellent support for saving fuel and cutting down unhealthy pollution (carbon footprints) in overcrowded cities, together with promoting exercise for millions of citizens pedaling rather than pushing the foot-pedal in a "gas-guzzling" vehicle.

As a bonus, bicycle "parking lots" take up less space by far than parking lots for autos—even the ones in Japan that have individual "lifts" raising one row of cars above the other over each parking space!

Shinkansen

The "shinkansen"—high-speed rail system—is the premium way to travel in Japan. In fact, any kind of rail system is the most convenient way to do so—and there are several variations. There are "regular" trains, which travel at about half the speed of the high-speed trains—but "speed,"—nevertheless. Then there are subways, which in some busy urban stations are built at two underground levels below the ground level station. And, in some rural areas there are two-car diesel-powered trains—almost "Toonerville Trolley" types. Plus, of course, buses in both urban and rural areas serving local residents' needs.

High speed rail train

Our family utilized all of them one time or another during our two weeks in Japan. When riding on a streamlined "shinkansen" train at near 100 miles-per-hour the sound and sensation when meeting another train on parallel tracks is that of a loud explosion caused by air pressure of the two trains running in opposite directions. I noted that the schedules of trains meeting each other seemed to avoid doing so at high speed inside tunnels—and there are many of them in mountainous Japan, as well as a few undersea between islands, as we experienced traveling from Kyoto on the main island of Honshu to Fukuoka on the southern island of Kyushu.

It's an amazing system!

All the comforts of home—at 100 m.p.h.

Geisha – or Not?

The day's schedule included a visit to the Silver Pagoda in Kyoto. It stood beautifully on the side of a mountain visible for miles. It almost felt like walking again as many miles after getting off public transportation and hoofing the last l-o-n-g hillside on foot up a narrow street lined with shop after shop selling souvenirs or trinkets of every kind.

Suddenly there was a lot of excitement and we noticed a number of young ladies dressed as geisha also walking up the hill. There was almost instant information among us tourists—Japanese and foreign—that they were "undergraduate" geisha, still learning the routines of professional entertainment in usually exclusive expensive geisha houses. And they were not bashful about having their pictures taken with people along the streets.

Surrounded by Americans

Good Eatin'

McDonald Restaurants in every city and town in Japan, with lines of waiting customers extending beyond the front doors out onto the sidewalk! Colonel Sanders standing along the street inviting guests in for Kentucky Fried Chicken! Or unique above-the-entrance signs touting fried pork or beef dishes inside!

What an invitation!

Or a singing waitress inviting guests to enter for a delicious meal! Or shop windows displaying "fake" dishes loaded with porcelain, price-tagged, likenesses of the menu items inside! They're all part of food establishments tempting hungry shoppers looking for a place to eat!

A meal in a ramen soupbowl!

And, among them all, in Sapporo, which we called home in Japan for ten years, a sign advertised "Paul's Café!" What a surprise to see a café with my name on it! Since it was there, we stopped in for lunch and inquired who "Paul" might have been or where he was from. The waiters informed us that Paul came from Western Europe (Belgium or Holland) some years ago and opened the café to bring that kind of "atmosphere" to the city. We did not hesitate to appreciate it, ordering a beer with our lunchtime sandwich!

Colonel Sanders' helper Mark   **Paul's Café**

Tree Trimmers

Temples, shrines and castles hundreds of years old and surrounding grounds to match! Those are some of the memories of any tourists visiting Japan, especially in ancient cities like Kyoto. Keeping them in "mint condition" obviously takes a great deal of care. One of the oldest most famous Buddhist temples covering an acre or so of land was completely covered by a steel framework and roof-above-the-roof during renovation, which was underway as we visited.

An interesting sidelight was that as we walked through the shiny-clean hallways in our stocking feet I noted two large wooden collection boxes for gifts by visitors. One was for funds toward costs of the renovation. The other was marked "For the poor and hungry of the world." An interesting combination of appeals!

Walking under the huge pine trees on the park-like grounds of the Nijo-jo Castle revealed another "surprise." At the very top of the trees were two men trimming branches to enhance the perfect shape and proportions of the trees!

Kyushu Interlude

Despite living in Japan for 16 years, none of the Strege family had ever visited Kyushu, the large southern island. We had lived in Hokkaido, the northern island, and on many occasions been to Tokyo and other places on the central island, Honshu. In fact, John and Mary were born in a hospital in Tokyo. But the southern islands of Shikoku and Kyushu were "out of range."

So our "tour director," John, was sure to include Kyushu on our itinerary, even though limited to only one day. On the round trip from Kyoto to Fukuoka, our train passed through other well-known cities like Hiroshima, and "crossed" the sea between islands—not over a bridge—but through an undersea tunnel. We arrived in Fukuoka, the northern most city on the island, midmorning, and made a walking tour of landmarks on John's map. There was appreciable construction and renovation work going on in this major industrial metropolis, and at the sports complex in one of the major parks we observed athletes apparently training to compete in the Beijing, China, Olympic Games later in the summer.

After lunch we headed back to the railroad station for a leisurely return to Kyoto. It was a day away from some of the "rushed" schedule of preceding days, and at the end of the day it was "mission accomplished!" We had finally set foot in Kyushu!

With apologies to the people of Rio de Janeiro, Brazil, and their statue of Christ the Redeemer, Joy extends her arms over the people of Fukuoka, Japan.

Kotoni

A day of re-living the past!! Kotoni is the Sapporo suburb where our family lived from 1958-65 while the four children on this trip went to Hokkaido International School. We rode the train from the Sapporo to the Kotoni stations. Everything is changed! Even the names of some of the streets, including the one where our home was located—Bunka-dori (Culture Lane)! Fortunately, when we mentioned the name to the taxi driver, he knew where to take us.

We walked the streets and alleys in every direction. Our home no longer exists. There is a new modern replacement. We only recognized two or three buildings from our era. What were empty lots are all built up with residences or commercial buildings.

The street where we lived

Mary in front of site of our house, yard and garden

Walking Bunka-dori toward the mountains we could see the skeleton of the ski-jumping structure from the 1970 Winter Olympics, held in the Sapporo area a few years after we moved away. We recognized the sign of the family doctor who provided medicines for the children's aches and pains, but the building seemed vacant on the Saturday morning we were there. A new Lutheran Church built a few blocks from our home was locked because it is currently without a pastor. But the little candy store at the end of Bunka-dori where it meets a major thoroughfare was still there, and we bought a few samples for old time's sake!

When we stopped in front of a building which appeared possibly to be at the site of the neighborhood bathhouse during our days, (cf story in "How Near is Near?" p.123) a lady opened the door to check why seven Americans would be gathering in the street in front of her home. When I asked her in Japanese about the bathhouse the children remembered from 30 years ago, she informed us that it had been moved and rebuilt several blocks away, and following an old kindly custom which we experienced many times when we lived in the neighborhood, she not only told us how to get to the new bathhouse, but put on her shoe-slippers and personally walked with us to the address. What kindness! -- We didn't really regret that it was closed for business that Saturday morning!

Reminiscing about the morning could go on and on—and probably happens on occasion in our respective homes!!!

Dollar Stores

Americans who travel to far-away countries—whether their "homeland" or not—usually seek out bargains for gifts to take home as reminders of the visit. The Strege family was no exception. And whether because of frugality or whatever, "Dollar Stores" were especially attractive. At the time of our visit, signs above the doors beckoned: "100 YEN SHOP." Interestingly, during this trip to Japan the international currency exchange rate was just at 100 yen equaling one dollar. And whether in the largest cities like Tokyo or Kyoto, or small towns like Yoichi, the traveling Streges were drawn in.

Without exaggerating, I can say there were bargains galore. Even this octogenarian picked up a box of 1,200 toothpicks for

Y100. The most recent ones I had bought in St. Louis prior to the trip was a box of 250 for 40 cents, about $2.00 for 1,200.

Common to both boxes were the words in fine print: "Made in China." – Maybe it's the shipping cost that doubles the price!!!

A Dream to Remember -- Yoichi

It was a dream come true when it happened in our early years in Japan.

Our family of two—Vercile and I—were among the first Lutheran couples to be assigned to serve in Hokkaido, the northern island of Japan after World War II. As more families

39

arrived and grew with the addition of children, there was a felt need for vacation facilities "closer to home" than the retreat centers serving missionaries in Tokyo and areas even farther to the south, hundreds of miles from Hokkaido.

A gift from a mission group in the U.S. resulted in location of a beautiful beach area along the shores of the Sea of Japan available for a 20-year lease, and the erection of two vacation homes to serve the needs of the Hokkaido families.

The 20-year lease has long since expired and the houses have been dismantled, but the Strege children returning to see the "old haunts" decades later were not going to be denied going back to revive wonderful memories of Hokkaido vacations long ago.

As we walked back to the locale from the Yoichi railroad station we found the beach profoundly changed. The removal of beach sand over the decades to be used for highway construction and other purposes has changed the beach to a long row of huge concrete blocks to protect the shore line from the ravages of storm waves. But some of the scenery was still there, and the memories of happier days was revived by the presence of a young lady and her 5-year old son visiting the area the same time we were.

When the mother—a complete stranger—heard our story of memories of those days, she excused herself briefly, ran off to some newer beach houses set farther back from the water, and came back with a bowl of freshly picked cherries to share with our family. On the Strege side, Keith, who has a hobby of collecting U.S.$2 bills, reciprocated by giving a $2 bill to the 5-year old boy.

International relations were enhanced that day!

People and beach lines change over 45 years (1963, 2008), but the mountain backdrop does not change.

A Miracle

Four hotel rooms were reserved to accommodate our "family" of seven travelers in Japan every evening: double rooms for Ruth and Keith (husband and wife), John and Mark (brothers), Mary and Joy (mother and daughter), and a single room for me (grandpa). The routine was to gather in one of the larger rooms to reminisce about the day's experiences, relax with a snack and a drink or two, and finally head off to our rooms for a night's rest, to meet the next morning at breakfast together.

It was one of our last nights in Sapporo, and after getting back to my room down the hall a ways, I got ready to take my nightly shower. It was a large bathtub/shower arrangement, and after I got lathered up under the shower, suddenly my feet slipped out from under me and I felt myself falling backwards out of the tub! What a myriad of thoughts flash through your mind in a few seconds in that kind of emergency! How and when will the kids find me? Will it be because they miss me at breakfast? How will they get into my room—I have the only key? What will they do with the body—if beyond hospitalization? Is it worth shipping back to the U.S.? And what about the shower—it's still running?

All that in a few seconds, only to find myself lying on the floor with one leg still hanging over the edge into the bathtub! And I felt no pain! Obviously I missed hitting the washbasin and the toilet bowl or even a wall or the door in this compact room! I was lying on the shower curtain under me, which was torn from all but a few of the snaps on the rod above, and apparently cushioned my fall, and some of the spray from the shower was pelting my face. Assuming no broken bones nor feeling any major bruises, I got up from the floor, crawled back into the shower, snapped a few of the curtain rings back on the rod, and washed the rest of the soap off my body.

The next morning after breakfast, I invited John to my room to help snap the rest of the curtain onto the shower rod, and we resumed the rest of our planned visit to Japan!

Reflecting on the experience, it was a miracle! What was God trying to tell me at age 83? Does He think I'm still worth having around? If there's an answer, I'm still waiting to find out what it is!

(P.S. When I was a boy and one of us children spun a tale that seemed unbelievable, one of the others threw out the challenge:

"Cross your heart, and hope to die?" This unbelievable story prompts me to say: "Cross my heart, and hope to die." It is a true story! It happened! But, sorry, I have no photos of the bathroom to prove it.)

Sapporo TV Tower

Everybody referred to it as "Terebee Toe" (The TV Tower) when we lived in Sapporo in the 1960's. Situated in the center of "downtown," it served several purposes besides being the transmission tower for television. About a third of its height from the top, it housed an enclosed observation platform standing at one end of the city-block-wide floral park stretching toward the mountains in the distance. An elevator transported visitors to the platform area, which also featured a number of souvenir shops. And at ground level it was the central transfer point for the busy bus system—a sort of bus terminal—from which passengers could reach almost all sections of the city. Every day during the school year our children changed busses there at the juncture of the lines between our home and their school.

Sapporo TV Tower and 130-year old Clock Tower

When our family group visited again 50 years later the embellished tower and the beautiful flower filled central city park were still in place, while the transportation system's transfer point moved mostly to the subway level below everything else. But the memories were vividly relived as we walked the streets not far away where the historic 130 year-old "clock tower," (upgraded by the lighted digital clock high on the TV Tower) and other landmarks of the city remain.

As a sidelight, we could hardly miss noting other cities we visited—Tokyo and Kyoto—also have their own TV/Observation Towers.

View from TV Tower Looking Toward Mountains

Musicians Reunion – 50 Years Later

Teacher and students, that is!

In 1958 our family moved back to Hokkaido from Tokyo. Daughter Ruth was in 2nd grade, and we bought a new Yamaha made piano so she could take piano lessons. Her teacher, "Dick" Kurokawa, whom we knew from our previous service in Sapporo eight years earlier, had meanwhile done graduate study in music at the University of Missouri in Columbia, MO, and earned the Japanese title of "Sensei" applied to teachers, pastors, doctors and other professional graduates. We were happy to learn that he lived within walking distance from our new home in Sapporo, and Ruth could walk to his home for lessons.

Interestingly, Ruth's younger brother, John, not yet in school, after observing her practicing her piano lessons, would climb onto the piano bench and play what she was practicing. Apparently he had a proclivity toward music, and it wasn't long until both Ruth and John were students of Kurokawa Sensei. Years later, in college in Chicago, John majored and earned his Master's Degree in music.

Our 2008 family trip to Japan took us back to Sapporo, and what excitement for Ruth and John to meet now retired Kurokawa Sensei once again. He and John, especially, were thrilled to exchange experiences after 50 years!

John and his piano teacher of 50 years ago

45

Strege Kicked the Door In

It was the fourth formal reception of our two-week visit in Japan. We worshipped in the sanctuary of Sapporo Central Lutheran Church on the 7th floor of a building erected in downtown Sapporo just blocks from the Sapporo Tower in 1975 after merger of three smaller congregations. Pastor Kumei welcomed Vercile and me when we visited 13 years ago in 1995, and welcomed the Strege family now in 2008 not only as pastor of the congregation, but also as newly elected president of the national Japan Lutheran Church.

President Kumei leads worship at altar   **90 year old Kamo Sensei**

After worship we were escorted to a large hall for a potluck reception featuring a whole line up of exotic Japanese sushi dishes provided by the 40 to 50 members present. As the meal progressed a series of persons took the microphone for speeches of reminiscing and welcome. Finally the mike was handed to the oldest person present, 90 year old Kamo Sensei. She had been kindergarten director of Grace Lutheran Church where I was pastor from 1958-1962. The climax of her reminiscing about our working together was about a day when the door to the kindergarten somehow was jammed and I was successful in kicking it in so we could enter. Frankly, I had forgotten it ever

46

happened, but she had the crowd roaring as she recalled what she thought was one of the funniest happenings of her career.

And it was moments like these among others of a serious nature that made this two-week visit such an exciting experience for our family!

Bountiful Blessings

Names, names, names! Some came back easily. Others seemed to have slipped away. At the reception in Sapporo there was Mr. Ujie, who was president of Grace (Megumi) congregation when I was called to assume the post of East Asia Area Secretary in 1962, Pastor Osawa who entered the seminary during my earlier years in Japan, and Mr. Murakami, a school-teacher who reminded me of his visit in our home in St. Louis in the 1960's.

Greetings from numerous Sapporo friends

Master of Ceremonies was Dr. Narita, current president of the Center congregation and a Senior Professor at Hokkaido University who recalls Sunday School during my early years in Sapporo, and whose wife served as English translator for international global leaders at the "G-8 Summit" in Hokkaido the week after our visit. Near the end of the festivities Dr. Narita arranged presentation to me of a spring cherry blossom painting by a well-known Japanese artist, which now hangs on a wall in my home.

Painting Presentation

Meanwhile, Mrs. Matsuo reminded me of my presiding at her wedding some 45 years ago when she prophesied to me that her non-Christian groom would eventually become a Christian, updated me about her grown Christian sons when I visited Sapporo in 1995 and now updated me on her entire Christian family in 2008!

Numerous others whose names I cannot recall gathered around me at the reception to share memories from the past. At the end of the afternoon my response was to praise God for bountiful blessings bestowed over many years!

You Baptized Me 50 Years Ago!

It was the last full day of our two-week visit in Japan. We had already spent several days in Sapporo where the family lived from 1958 to 1965. The "schedule" called for a visit to Asahigawa, 100 miles to the north, where Vercile and I lived between 1950 and 1956, during which time John and Mary were born. But a degree of "family fatigue" was developing and the children—who all "grew up" in Sapporo—were anxious to spend another day "researching" old familiar places rather than making a trip by train (we had "done" quite a few trains in the past two weeks!) to a city they had never really known and in a sense had more meaning for me than for them. So John suggested that he rent a car and drive me to Asahigawa for the day while the rest of the family group spent another day in Sapporo.

Japanese autos have "right-hand drive" rather than "left-hand drive" like we do in the U.S., but John immediately adjusted to driving on the left side of streets and highways, and the two of us had an exhilarating trip on the new (to me) super-highway to Asahigawa on a gorgeous spring day on the beautiful northern island of Hokkaido!

Arriving at the outskirts of Asahigawa, I discovered that 50+ years after Vercile and I moved away, I saw nothing familiar and was happy John had checked out the map to find the location of St. Paul Lutheran Church. Having phoned him before arriving, we were greeted at the door by Pastor Miyazawa, whom I had never met before. After a tour of the beautiful new ferro-concrete building which replaced the old frame building erected in 1951 (see story on p. 90 of my book, "How Near is Near?") the pastor invited us to lunch in the new City Hall across the street, also unfamiliar.

Paul and John at entrance of new Asahigawa St. Paul Lutheran Church

After lunch Pastor Miyazawa inquired whether there was anything else I would like to see. Remembering that in my early ministry I had reached out to the area of the city occupied by a settlement of the aboriginal Ainu Japanese (comparable to Native Americans in the U.S.—cf. "How Small is Small?" p.78), I asked whether we could visit "the Ainu village." He informed me that it no longer existed in the same style, but that there was a museum-like exhibit area, to which he drove us in his car.

Among a set of model homes, buildings and implements from the ancient Ainu civilization, there were three large roofed outdoor souvenir shops. As I walked toward them, a woman came out from behind the central shop. She somehow recognized me, called out my name "Strege," and said in Japanese: "You baptized me 50 years ago and, remember, we had a Sunday school in my home for neighborhood children?" I couldn't believe it!! It was one of the most moving experiences of my visit in Japan!

"You baptized me 50 years ago!"

According to my calculations, I would place her baptism back closer to 55 years, than 50 years ago. And she was among as many as half-a-dozen persons I met again on this trip, whom I had been privileged to baptize 45 to 55 years ago! God's name be praised!

Land of the Rising Sun

From time immemorial Japan has prided itself on being "The Land of the Rising Sun." It is located at the east end of the Asian landmass in such a position that when the sun rises every morning west of the International Date Line in the Pacific Ocean, it is first seen on the islands of Japan. And what can be more exciting and inspiring than that first sighting of the brilliant sun rising above the horizon in the east!

But the accompanying photo seems to betray that brilliance. It was taken not of the rising sun, but of the setting sun above the mountains of Sapporo on Japan's northern island the last evening of our visit there in 2008. Sadly, I witnessed that it looked the same in the mornings as I observed the sunrise out of the window of my hotel room facing east A haze in the air blotted out some of the sun's brightness.

As is true in many places in the world the air quality over Japan, including Sapporo, has deteriorated appreciably in recent

51

decades due to industrial air pollution. Aware of the problem already for a long time, the Japanese have been working hard to counter this phenomenon, but only with partial success.

Purifying the air is a challenge not only in Japan, but globally, and will require the cooperation of every industrialized nation from America to Europe to China and everywhere between and beyond. To the extent that it is successful Japan will bask again in bright sunrises to reclaim pride in being the land of the rising sun!

PART 2   Grandchildren Reminisce and Reflect

"Ask, and you will receive," is not only a promise in the Bible, but proved true, also, when I asked my 18 grandchildren whether they would be willing to contribute a story to this book. All 18 responded, a number of them submitting more than one story!

It just so happens that their age range is 18 years, from the oldest at 30 and the youngest at 12. They are identified by their first names with their stories. As further identification, their names are listed below by families of my six children, which occur according to their ages, eldest to youngest.

Ruth and Keith Forni	Mark and Diane Strege
Andrew (Drew)	Seth
Adam	Ashley
Aaron	Luke
John and Beth Strege	Tim and Gail Strege
Tara - spouse John Slawinski	Zachariah (Zack)
Faith - spouse Lonnie Colson	Joseph (Joe)
Hayley	Rachel
Leah - spouse Eric Huffman	
Mary and Ron Petry	Lois and Tom Dolan
Christopher (Chris)	Joshua (Josh)
Joy	Matthew (Matt)
	Benjamin (Ben)

The stories by the grandchildren are not in the order of their ages, but appear in random order.

The Nose Thing – by Tara

I have a lot of stories about growing up in the Strege family. One that sticks out in my mind is, as I call it, "the nose thing."

My first memory about it was in St. Louis at Grandma and Grandpa's house. Some of us were sitting around the kitchen table. I don't remember who all was there except I remember Great-Grandma Petzoldt was there. She was playing pinochle, and was trying to teach me, but I really wasn't getting it. All of a sudden she put her finger up next to her nose! I followed just because everyone else was doing it.

I found out it was a little contest to see who was the last one to put their finger next to their nose. I know this little thing sounds crazy, but we did it all of the time! Every time we were in St. Louis we would do it. I remember Grandma Strege would get into it while she was standing over the stove or something, and normally she was the last one to do it.

Paul with sons John, Tim, and Mark in January 2009.

What's funny is that my younger sister, Faith, got married some 20+ years later, in January 2009. We were all sitting around the table talking, and we did "the nose thing," and, unfortunately, Grandpa lost.

It's funny how such a small little thing will bring up so many wonderful memories from my childhood.

My First Arch Experience! – by Drew

One of my fondest memories of visiting Grandpa & Grandma as a really young kid was visiting the St. Louis Arch! I quite vividly recall entering the white & silver "pod" (which was the elevator) and being in a state of awe looking a bit uneasily at

54

Grandma, Grandpa, Mom, Dad and Adam (Aaron wasn't born yet). I think Adam was less intimidated, but I was slightly freaked out because of the unknown results of how high we were going in this spaceship-like small pod. My uneasiness was soothed by Mom, Dad & Grandpa & Grandma's confidence.

Once we were at the top, I thought the craziest thing was the floor! It was actually arched! I had never walked on something like this and looking out of the windows was very cool, realizing we were actually INSIDE the top of this completely unique structure that I had seen a number of times before, every time we would approach Grandpa & Grandma Strege's house. It was the visual reference point that we were finally here, after the 5+hr. drive from Chicago. The Arch trip is burned into my brain and I'm thankful for that experience!

How Smart Is Smart? – by Seth

Getting good grades in school has always been important in the Strege family. My Grandpa likes to tell the story that both he and Grandma were valedictorians at their high schools. Grandpa always mentions that Grandma's graduation class was much larger than his. She graduated from Roosevelt High School in St. Louis and Grandpa graduated from a small school in rural Kansas.

I graduated with a 4.0 GPA and was valedictorian at St. Charles West High School. When my father announced to Grandpa that I was also a valedictorian he was very impressed and replied, "It seems to run in the family." Then, when my father mentioned that he worked hard in high school only to end up with a B+ average my Grandpa immediately remarked, "I guess it skipped a generation!"

What Do You Want to be When You Grow Up? – by Joy

"What do you want to be when you grow up?" It seems like children are constantly asked this question by parents, relatives, and teachers, throughout their childhood. Most children answer with something like a firefighter or a princess - usually occupations that they can act out in imaginary play. Even as kids get older in their grade school years, when asked that question, most kids will still respond with something that they may never end up actually doing in their lives.

I was in fourth grade when we had to do a class project about what we wanted to be when we grew up. It was shortly after Grandma had her first major stroke and my mom had gone to stay with my grandparents for a little while to help out. I remember talking to my mom while she was in St. Louis and she told me about the occupational therapy that Grandma was receiving to help her get back to doing some of the things she wanted to do around the house, such as cooking and cleaning.

As my mom continued to describe the therapy in more detail, I began thinking that it sounded like something I would love doing. So when the project came up in class a couple weeks later, I immediately thought about occupational therapy. I went around my fourth grade class saying, "I want to be an occupational therapist when I grow up!" to which everyone responded with, "what is an occupational therapist?" I explained to them that my grandma had a stroke and the occupational therapist was working with her so that she could continue to do all of the daily activities she needed to around the house and in the community.

Now, 14 years later, as I am getting my master's degree in occupational therapy, people still ask me, "What is an occupational therapist?" Fortunately, I now have a better answer than, "they help people learn how to cook and clean after a stroke." But every time I'm asked that question, I still think back to the time when I originally learned about occupational therapy. I think about how important it was to Grandma to have her independence around the house and continue in her greatly valued roles as wife, mother, and grandmother. There are a lot of ways in which Grandma has been an inspiration to all of us grandchildren over the years; this is just one way in which she influenced my life. It was unfortunate that she had the stroke, but that is what led me to discover my passion of occupational therapy.

The slogan for the field of occupational therapy is "Living life to its fullest!" I think Grandma really embodied that spirit in living a long and rich life in which she touched so many people's lives in a meaningful way. Our family has a history of serving people in our communities, from pastors to nurses to teachers and so on; I hope to use my career to continue in the tradition.

St. Louis Band Trip & Busch Stadium - by Drew

From the 5th grade through university, I was massively involved in music performance and playing the trombone in numerous bands (jazz, symphonic, marching, orchestral, combos, etc.). To this day, that solid background in music has given me an excellent edge in my current fields of DJ-ing and TV & Film editing in Hollywood, CA.

One time in about 1992, we had an All-City (Joliet, IL) Band trip to St. Louis for a Midwest competition performance. I remember getting special permission to meet Grandpa at the Union Station mall on one of our "group outings" during the trip. I still have this really cool blue & black "St. Louis" hat from that mall that Grandpa bought for me as a gift on that trip. I recall walking around with Grandpa with a VIP feeling that I was able to break away from the group to go off with family for a while! After we had a great lunch and spent some quality time together, we parted ways.

Our itinerary included a St. Louis Cardinals game. I don't believe I had actually ever been there before this trip. I thought it was a cool ballpark; however, growing up in Chicago, I had Cubs blood running through my veins. I have only become more of a die-hard Cubs fan since then, but didn't realize the rivalry that would become clearer to me over the years of watching baseball. If you are unfamiliar with the NL Central, one thing you can't be is a St. Louis Cardinals fan and a Chicago Cubs fan at the same time. Although I love my St. Louis based side of the family, we generally stay away from baseball talk!

Toy Story – by Zack

I have played many games at Grandpa's house over the years. Some of the toys and games were introduced to me by my dad, because they were his as a child. One such toy is the play-buoy. It consists of two long ropes covered with wax, with handles on each end, and a buoy with a hole down the center in which the cables run through. Many years ago my Uncle Mark and my father Tim demonstrated how to use this to my cousin Seth and me. A person stands at each end and holds the two handles at each end together. One person yanks his hands apart and the buoy zips toward the other person at a high rate of speed. The other person does the same thing, and the cycle repeats. It was scary, but fun.

One other game that I loved at Grandpa's house was a puzzle in the shape of an arrow. It contained five pieces: a square, a large triangle, a small triangle, and two oddly shaped polygons. I would take all the pieces out and put them back into the container to complete the puzzle. Upon completing the puzzle I would put it away until the next time when I visited Grandpa and I would do it again. After about five times my dad told me that it is possible to make a square out of all the pieces as well. This was much more challenging than the original puzzle. I eventually memorized that puzzle as well. If I pull out that puzzle today I can complete it and complete the square after fiddling around with the pieces for about a minute.

I like many other games and toys at Grandpa's. Some of them are the rocking horse, lawn darts, the Sticky Wicket, the Wizzer top, Gnip Gnop, Battling Tops, Tip It, The Fish Bait game, Basket, Zig-Zag-Zoom, Uncle Wiggly, Scan, the Hippity Hop, Grandpa's clothes chute, and Air Hockey. I also enjoy playing chess or checkers with Grandpa. Going to Grandpa's house always was and is fun.

One Way – by Joy

For as long as I can remember there has been a puzzle in the same spot in Grandma and Grandpa's living room. It sits in the drawer of a table between two sitting chairs, Grandma's on one side and Grandpa's on the other. The table does not have any other games or puzzles in it, so I am not sure how this little puzzle made it into that drawer and has stayed there all these years. The puzzle consists of a small plastic tray with five colored pieces of various shapes and sizes. On the front of the tray it says, "There is only ONE WAY to make a square out of these 5 pieces."

This puzzle brings back a memory of one time when my brother, Chris, and I were staying with my grandparents for a couple days. My brother, who always had a very determined personality, decided one day that we were going to solve that puzzle! Being the young children that we were, this was a difficult task we were about to undertake. So Grandma sat down at the kitchen table with us to work on it. We diligently tried fitting the shapes together, but could not quite make a *perfect* square. It seemed like forever that we were sitting at the table concentrating. But just as we were about to give up, we finally solved it! We felt like we had really accomplished something big. Consequently, when it was time to put the puzzle back away, we became concerned we might forget how we had solved it and be back to square one. So just to humor us for all the hard work we had put in, Grandma got out a piece of paper and traced out the pieces to make an "answer key" to the puzzle, putting our young minds at ease.

Ever since that day, whenever I visit Grandma and Grandpa's house I always go to the drawer in the living room and get out the "One Way" puzzle. I don't know what ever happened to the "answer key" we made that day, but luckily I never needed it after that. Sometimes I just check to see if the puzzle is still there, and other times I actually take it out and play with it for a bit. But in any case, throughout my entire life that little puzzle has always been in its place in the drawer.

I started reflecting on why this simple little puzzle stuck in my mind so strongly over all these years. I realized the puzzle itself was fairly meaningless, but it was the consistency of it always being there in the drawer that was meaningful to me. Like most things in my grandparents' house (the Dr. Seuss books on the shelf, the wedding photos down the hallway, the beer can collection in the basement, just to name a few), I knew that every time I went to visit them, that puzzle would be sitting right where I expected it. The consistency of it always being there seemed to have a nostalgic effect. Of course the "One Way" puzzle has become increasingly easy over the years, but that has not stopped me from continuing to enjoy it!

From Pancakes to Chile – by Hayley

Produce Patch, Dollar Store, Cookies, Ted Drewes' Frozen Custard, and PANCAKES. All of these come to mind when I think of visiting Grandma and Grandpa Strege. I felt so guilty because the first thing I thought of before Grandma Strege died was PANCAKES! In the morning after a good night's sleep in the bed with the flowered bedspread, Grandma would ask us which character we wanted for our pancake design: Mickey or Minnie Mouse, Donald or Daisy Duck. Grandpa would come around with the Blue Bonnet margarine from the large tub and give us the character's facial features: nose, eyes, mouth, earrings. I miss those moments with both of them. I wish I had shown them, and especially my deceased Grandma, how much I loved them, even if I expressed that through Grandma's yet-unmatched buttermilk pancakes.

Now I long for the more personal testimonials of my missionary grandparents. I didn't know Grandpa was fluent in Japanese until I was about twenty years old. Or, that he knew Lutherans in Chile, South America. Who knew that after nearly two decades of eating buttermilk pancakes in that yellow-floored kitchen, drinking water poured from a half-gallon milk jug, that I would spend five incredible months in the very country (Chile) whose lovely people sent my Grandpa an embroidered figure of gratitude that continues to hang on the kitchen wall in his home!

Dios nos ama a todos y realmente es una bendición tener abuelos cuyos corazones resuenan con el espíritu misionero.

I am convinced that my desire to teach English in a Latin American country has been largely shaped by the influence of my missionary-minded grandparents. (Even though it all started with buttermilk pancakes!)

Not Just Pancakes – by Chris

I think every grandchild has at least one thing that they are secretly uber excited for when they visit Grandma and Grandpa's house and for me it was the pancakes. Every morning when it was time to "Rise and shine!" I was invariably asked by Grandma, "What do you want for breakfast?" and I would always answer, "Can I have some pancakes please?" Now, one might think that the conversation would end there, but once upon a time when I was very young Grandma made the mistake of voluntarily making me a *Mickey Mouse* pancake. I, of course, thought this was the coolest thing ever, and from then on the next question had to be, "What kind of pancakes?"

I soon began putting Grandma's pancake making skills to the test. Every visit I would push the envelope a little farther. I asked for *Donald Duck*, *Goofy*, etc. but she could soon make all the *Disney* characters with ease (and their female counterparts for my sister, which just consisted of making little pancake bows to put on top).

For those interested, Grandma really had the method mastered. The secret was to put all of the details in the pan first and then pour the head. This way all of the features were outlined in white, and of course they were just slightly darker than the rest of the head.

As I got older and entered my dinosaur phase, I thought I'd really push my luck one morning, and when asked what kind of pancakes I would like I hopefully replied, "Can you make a Stegosaurus?" After realizing how much I was looking forward to this Stegosaurus pancake, Grandma decided to try to understand what a Stegosaurus looked like. I don't remember if I had a book along with me or if I described it to her, but she agreed that she would try to make me a Stegosaurus. I had never asked for anything like this before, and I thought for sure she was going to fail miserably. However, I thought it was worth a shot, at the worst she would try a few times, which just meant there would be more pancakes to eat.

I waited anxiously at the table and then, smiling contently, Grandma set the Stegosaurus pancake in front of me, its tail hanging off the side of the plate. I could not believe it; it looked exactly like a Stegosaurus!

Although no words were spoken during the unveiling of this masterpiece, I think we both realized that there may have been a little luck involved and that this was about as far as we could take this ritual before we got some disappointing results.

I just asked for regular pancakes after that.

The Ice Storm – by Matthew

Ice. It was everywhere. Coating every tree, every road. We had no electricity; our only heat source was the fireplace. This was The Ice Storm of 2009.

Nobody saw it coming. It started sleeting Monday afternoon, while we were still in school. Everyone was hoping to have Tuesday off, but nobody thought we would miss two weeks of school. On Tuesday morning school had been cancelled, and there was a thin layer of ice on everything. Then, at about nine o'clock, the power went out. That night, round two began.

On Wednesday morning, everything had a half-inch coat of ice, even the smallest of twigs on the trees. Then the wind started blowing. Not very hard, but hard enough to start bringing limbs down. The nights were pitch black, because no lights were on to illuminate the frosty air. These were the scariest times. Every ten seconds, a huge branch could be heard going down somewhere in the woods, or on the street, or in the back yard. The next morning two trees had fallen across our road, completely blocking it. One of the neighbors had a chainsaw, so we set about clearing the road.

After that, hanging around with the neighbors became constant. Considering we had no electronic form of entertainment, we stuck together to keep each other company. Needless to say we made it through the ice storm by working together and keeping the faith.

Grandma's Tempura! – by Drew

Of all the super delicious amazing outrageously tasty food Grandma would make, my absolute, hands down, without question favorite was when we would have large family gatherings on Lonkar Dr. and "OPERATION: STREGE

TEMPURA" would be in full blazing effect. I would help sometimes with the chopping of veggies, but most of that work was done by the adults. My personal favorites would be the carrots and chicken. There was also plenty of broccoli, onions, zucchini, and other veggies.

As the operation was in effect, I believe the general process was chop the tempura raw ingredients, make the batter, dip tempura in the batter, and then place the tempura in the hot oil. The anticipation of the completion of this process was at the top of my brain while we (kids) were downstairs playing with (plastic) dart guns, and a plethora of amazing board games from the 60s & 70s.

Once Grandma, Grandpa and our Moms, Dads, Aunts, and Uncles were scooping out the tempura for them to cool, they would give us the green light and it was most definitely time to get down. I've never had better Tempura since, and doubt I ever will. Thanks Grandma & Grandpa for these unforgettable Tempura super special dinners. They will never be forgotten!

Chuck E Cheese's – by Ashley

I have always enjoyed going to Chuck E. Cheese's ever since I was a small child. When Grandpa found out how much I loved Chuck E. Cheese's he began sending us Chuck E. Cheese's coupons. Whenever someone in the family gets a birthday card or Christmas card from Grandpa there are always Chuck E. Cheese's coupons enclosed. At other times, he just sends us coupons or includes them with a newspaper "funnies" clip or a newspaper article clip that Grandpa wrote. Too bad there were no Chuck E. Cheese's Restaurants around when Grandpa was a child. But then again, you are never too old to enjoy Chuck E. Cheese's. The slogan says "Where a Kid Can Be a Kid." Perhaps it should be changed to "Where Anyone Can Be a Kid."

My Surprise Visit – by Faith

There are many fond memories when I think back to times spent in St. Louis with Grandma and Grandpa. Christmas cookies, pancakes, games in the basement…these are some of the first memories that come to mind. I also remember a family tradition of ours as we would drive down to St. Louis; as we approached the city, my sisters and I would be on the lookout for the arch, to see who could spot it first.

One particularly unique memory is the time I was surprised by a dog running down the hallway. Let me explain. When we would go to visit Grandma and Grandpa, we would often park in their driveway. If we parked in the street, we would always park behind the driveway (from the car's perspective). This location is what I was used to, and so naturally, I would walk directly to the driveway in front of the vehicle, and enter their house.

This day was different however. I am not sure why we parked in front of their driveway. Perhaps another family member had parked behind it. Whatever the reason, I didn't realize it at the time. All I knew was that we had parked on the street, and it was time to go in the house. Naturally, I walked to the driveway in front of the vehicle, and I entered the house. As I opened the screen door, I was startled to see a large dog running down the hall towards me. I was very confused, and I must have quickly shut the door, because the dog never reached me. I don't think it was until that moment that I realized I had gone to the wrong house! I had walked up the wrong driveway and entered the next-door neighbor's house.

Now, one thing I forgot to mention was that I had a childhood fear of dogs. I cannot remember how old I was when this happened, but I'm pretty sure I was young enough where I was still afraid. Thankfully, nothing else came of the event, and I just went back over to Grandma and Grandpa's house. I can still remember it, though, and how startled I was to see a dog running toward me.

This story of my misunderstanding is just one of the many memories from our trips to St. Louis to visit Grandma and Grandpa. There are many other memories I can recall, like the time Grandma and Grandpa took us all over St. Louis while our parents were away on vacation. In pondering what to write for Grandpa to include in his book, two things streamed through my head. First, many memories came to mind, and I sought to find one that was specific enough to write a story about. Second, I

64

thought how I wish I had gotten to know Grandma better. I am thankful for these happy memories, and I hope this one silly story brings back your own memories as well.

An Unexpected Surprise – by Rachel

I was at Lake Tablerock with my cousins, my aunt and uncle, my mom, my brother, and my grandpa several years ago.

We were out one day on their boat. Everyone was finally dried off, and out of the blue a huge wave crashed over our boat. My cousin Joy, taking no chances, stood up and braced herself. Two other waves also crashed over our boat.

When all the mayhem was over we were all soaked! Grandpa, who had been wearing clothes, looked like someone had dumped water all over him.

I will never forget how funny and crazy this day was!

Surprise Spider Nest in a Kayak – by Drew

At a family reunion during the week of June 19, 1993 (I have the exact date from a membership card I can't believe I just found!). All the Streges, Dolans, Petrys, and Fornis were at a massive family reunion celebration at the Lake of the Ozarks in Missouri.

Shortly after the cousins, brothers & I explored the available activities, Adam, Aaron, Chris and myself decided kayaking across the Lake of the Ozarks would be super radical. Side-note: These are single occupancy style kayaks - from your waist down your legs are inside a small hole with your legs inside. Twenty minutes in (ALMOST HALF WAY THERE- in the middle of the lake) we hear Chris yelling! I look over and he is smashing his kayak with his paddle as hundreds* of spiders are swarming his kayak from the manhole out! "SPIDERS!" he yells. SO with initial concern (that turned into hilarity) we all circled his kayak and assaulted a fury of paddle bashes to his kayak. INSANE, and HYSTERICAL! After the spiders were annihilated, we continued our way to the other side of the lake. Success!

*(probably dozens, but I recall hundreds)

Killer Waters - by Joshua

I have always been one to enjoy a good adrenaline rush. I like to do things that get my heart racing and leave me screaming with energy. When I heard that my church group would be traveling down to Tennessee to go white water rafting, I knew I was about to be in for the time of my life. What I didn't know was that this trip would also be one that I thought could be the end of my life.

The 5-hour trip down to the Ocoee River seemed to take forever, and everyone in the van was ready as ever to ride the rapids. We finally arrived at the cabin where we would meet our guides and go over the basic techniques needed to make the trip fun and safe. Everyone listened intently, or so it seemed, and finally the moment arrived to load up the rafts and head to the river. When we got there, the brightly colored rafts of all the various raft companies dotted the churning white water. We were all ready to get in and join in the action. As we carried our raft down to the entrance point, untamed excitement slowly began to turn into hushed fear as the swiftly moving water got closer and closer. The guide gave us one last review of all the paddling commands as we loaded in the raft and got into our positions. I chose to be in back for the first part, because there would be a chance to move around a little ways down the river. Everyone seemed to stop and hold their breath as the guide shoved us away from shore and started our journey down awesomely powerful rapids of the Ocoee.

Things started well, the raft gliding smoothly over the water, everyone doing all the commands in exact harmony. One raft from our group had a girl fall out in the first major rapid, a Class 2. Rapids are classified according to their intensity on a 1-6 scale, with 1 being simply swiftly moving water and 6 being perpetual suicide for anyone less than absolute expert. The section of Ocoee we were rafting contained levels 1-4, but had a particularly abundant amount of Class 4 rapids. Things continued to go well and we eventually got to some calm water where we had a chance to get out of the boat and swim a little or change positions on the raft. After the initial success of the trip, I was feeling gutsy and decided to take on the front left position. The front positions were a little more dangerous than the back, because you didn't have any raft in front of you. We decided to get going and I was ready as ever to continue on this adrenaline-pumping excursion in my new, and more intense, position on the raft.

As we started back downriver, the guide began to explain the next set of rapids. There were two Class 4 rapids, Table Saw and Diamond Splitter, pretty much right on top of each other. Hearing this got me pretty pumped. I was ready to face these two monsters, but then I began to realize that my front spot did not give me as much protection as the back. But hey, I'm no chicken, so I pushed it out of my mind. Big Mistake. As we approached Table Saw, my heart began beating uncontrollably as I saw the froth spewing into the air and heard the physical power of the water as it rushed over the smooth rock bed. In we went, but the back of the raft hung on a rock for a split second and that wonderful physical principle known as inertia betrayed me, throwing me off balance and out of the raft. No time to breathe, no time to get ready, just into the water I went, not knowing whether I would make it out alive or not. Now in this particular rapid, the water is only about two and a half feet deep, which is barely enough to cover me when I am lying down. As I fell out, my first thought was, I have to get up for air, or I am going to die. As my brain processed this thought, my neck shot up in an attempt to break the water and get much needed oxygen into my starving lungs. But something stopped me. Since I was in the front left, I fell out as the raft was going forward. The raft was on top of me, completely stopping any motion I made toward the surface. At this point, I know its over, my life is flashing before my eyes, my mind just going crazy with thoughts of the afterlife. When I think all is at its end, I feel a great weight lifted off me, and I can see light. It's the surface! And then what appear to be the hands of an angel reach down into the water and grab my life vest and yank me out of the water, where I immediately begin gasping for air. The guide screams at me to kick me feet to help get myself back into the raft. I did as she said and before I knew it, I was sitting in the floor of the raft, cold, confused, and happy to be alive. After a short rest, I reassumed a position on the raft, and trust me, it wasn't in the front! Everything after that little mishap went great and the trip was one of the best of my life.

Now, after a story like that, one might think that experience was enough to keep me away from these powerful waters, but that is where you would be wrong. I have returned to the Ocoee twice since, one of those times including another unlucky spill. But that is another story.

So, if any of you adrenaline junkies out there are looking for something to meet your need for excitement, I would highly recommend that you put your life in Mother Nature's hands and challenge the power of the Ocoee's killer white water!

Born In the USA – by Luke

"Born in the U.S.A." reminds people of different things. For instance, Bruce Springsteen wrote a hit song called "Born in the U.S.A." which talks about fighting in the war. To my father, "Born in the U.S.A." means something different. Grandpa and Grandma were missionaries in Japan and my father was their only child born in America. He was born in St. Louis while the family was visiting relatives on vacation. The other five children were all born in Japan.

My Grandpa used to always tell my father that he was the only child who could ever become President since you had to be born in America to become President. However, that is not the case. When I looked up the requirements for President on the internet I read that children born overseas to American citizens are eligible to run for president. So it turns out that all of my dad's brothers and sisters could also run for President. But it did make my dad feel special.

When I was in kindergarten I had the privilege of meeting President Bush. I even got a picture of him with his arm around me. For several years my dream was to become President of the United States. Because of the economy and other recent events, I no longer want to be president, but I am still proud to be born in the U.S.A.

I Got to Ghana before Obama – by Faith

Two years ago, I had the opportunity to go to Ghana, West Africa. A friend from college had been teaching at Bomso

68

Christian Academy but had to return to the States before the end of the school year. I volunteered to be her replacement for the last quarter of the year. I was 23 years old at the time, and not quite one year out of college. I was working at Starbucks at the time, so I had the freedom to give two weeks notice and get on the plane. I was attending church services regularly but had been thinking that I needed a spiritual kick in the butt. I thought this was an amazing opportunity that I didn't want to pass up. In fact, at the time, I knew that the church there taught and believed differently than I on some issues, but I figured that I knew what I believed and I didn't want to pass up the opportunity to teach in Africa.

While there, my job was to supervise a class of 16 students and to lead the running program for the students age 13 and up. I had boys and girls in my class, and their ages ranged from nine to sixteen years. The students wore uniforms, which seemed to be the norm in Ghana, from what I observed. The running program would meet at 6 A.M.; it was for exercise, not competition. There was a rule that if you showed up late in the morning, you would have to run at lunch, too. One day, I overslept and showed up at 6:15 A.M., so I ran at lunch to show them that I was accountable to the rule, too. I also had the opportunity to visit a couple of villages in Ghana, the beach in Ghana, and the country of Togo. From the job and these other experiences, I learned about poverty, education, and truth.

One of the experiences that is still striking to remember is the coexistence of poverty with modern technology and advertising. For example, in one city that we drove through there were dirt roads, and yet I saw a glass case filled with new cell phones. One village we drove past had mud houses with TV antennae attached. The city where we lived had areas with dirt roads and mud houses, and a billboard advertising an American hair product above one of the paved roads. Before I went, I think I had the conception that Africa had mud huts and famous animals like lions, elephants, and giraffes. After being there, I saw this strange mix of poverty with modern luxuries we have in this country.

I also saw a lot of poverty in the villages we visited. We saw two villages in Ghana and one in Togo (the names of which I cannot remember) that did not have a lot of the modern amenities we enjoy in this country. The village in Togo did consist of one-room mud huts. There was a witch doctor, and we saw idols that people had made and placed in front of their houses. It is strange that right now, as I am writing this story on my computer in my house, there are people in Togo living in those same mud huts. The poverty and pagan religion of Togo make it very different from here.

Another area, which I learned about, was education. I remember at a nearby village, I saw a church as we were walking through. I asked the friend who was leading us if that church taught the kids to read the Bible for themselves. He said no. One of the students at our school told me that in Ghana, some people go to Bible school to make money. She said people in the churches give their money, and they do not know that they are being deceived. I don't remember how she phrased it, but I got the distinct impression that 1, people go to Bible school for the wrong reason, and 2, people attend services and give money, unaware that they are being deceived. Recently, I was reminded of her statements when the preacher spoke of this verse in Romans 16: 17-18:

> Now I urge you, brethren, note those who cause divisions and offenses, contrary to the doctrine which you learned, and avoid them. For those who are such do not serve our Lord Jesus Christ, but their own belly, and by smooth words and flattering speech deceive the hearts of the simple.

The reason I mention the story about the village, and the comments of the student, are because both of them gave me a better appreciation for the importance of education. The school where I worked taught students English, reading, writing, math, and the basic school subjects. The students learned to read the Bible, and had memory work assigned. A basic education is fundamental not only to having job skills but also to overcome ignorance. That is why it was sad to hear of the village church that did not teach the children to read the Bible for themselves, or of the people who go to Bible school to make money, or of people being deceived.

When people are given a basic education, they can think and reason for themselves. Children can learn not only the practical skills they need to function as adults, but they can also train their minds to think about truth. Instead of being told what to think, they learn to think for themselves.

I suppose the biggest challenge, and the one I am most thankful for, was to seek the truth. Shortly after arriving in Ghana, the preacher/principal talked to me about knowing *why* you believe what you believe. He said some people preach to a group and want to baptize everyone; but when one of those baptized is faced with persecution, how will he stand up to it if he does not know why he believes? He challenged me to think about why I believe what I believe. When I went to Ghana, I felt strongly about what I believed, but I didn't really know why I believed it. Being there challenged me to ask the question *why*, and to find an answer. That challenge to seek the truth started there in Ghana, but I still had a lot of questions when I came home to the States. I studied the Bible intensively because I wanted to find the answers to my questions. I wondered why there were so many different denominations if they all claimed that the Bible was the truth? What does the Bible say? What is the Truth?

The time and the challenges in Ghana sparked the fire in me to find the answers to my questions. I guess you could say that I got the spiritual kick in the butt that I thought I needed, but it was different than what I expected. I thought that I needed a kick in the butt to see the importance of serving, of devotion, of commitment in serving God. I did see this while there, but in addition to it my whole outlook on faith and truth was changed. When I returned home I was able to do a systematic Bible study and find the answers to my questions. I was shocked to find out that I had been wrong in some of the things I had believed. Studying the Bible and seeing how I had believed differently than what it said made me realize the importance of studying the Bible for myself. I learned the personal responsibility I have to study the Bible. Though I am still learning, I can now say what I believe and why because I have sought the truth and found answers in the Bible.

I am forever grateful for the experiences I had in Ghana, because they challenged me to seek the Truth. I am thankful that the school where I worked gives the students an education and teaches them to read the Bible. I am saddened that many places in Ghana do not. And I am saddened that though education is a basic right in America, many people never stop to ask themselves: Why do I believe what I believe? What is the Truth? I challenge you to ask these questions, and to seek out the Truth. For me, it took a trip to Africa; what will it take for you?

Ten Dollars Please – by Zack

After 72 years Grandpa is still a good driver. Grandpa started driving at the age of 13 when his father's eyesight started to worsen. To give perspective, that was the year of FDR's second inauguration and the year of the Great General Motors Strike. Since I live in St. Louis I am able to visit Grandpa often. I have been a passenger in his current and previous Hyundai many times, and I can attest to the fact that he is a good driver to this day (even though my dad says he never uses his brakes and almost drove off a shelf road in the Rocky Mountains).

John spoofed his dad with a cartoon birthday card in 1971.

In a recent conversation Grandpa told me that he had to get his license renewed before he turned 85. When he went to the DMV he told the worker that they should test people of his age to see if they are still capable drivers. She didn't really reply to the remark, but just said to hand over the ten dollars to pay for the new license.

Into The Woods – by Benjamin

The bike trail that John and I had chosen was called "The Eastern Loop," and it was eighteen miles long. There were stops and exits every four miles allowing bikers to shorten the loop. John and I had decided to go ahead and try the whole thing. We had traveled about eight miles when we started to get a little tired, so we pulled off onto a little trail that we thought was a rest stop. However, we were horribly mistaken.

We kept following the little trail hoping for a bench or a place to sit down. Finding nothing we just kept going, deciding that it would probably join back to "The Eastern Loop." We soon found ourselves off the beaten path and ended up by a small bridge and pool of water. We crossed the bridge only to find that it, too, led nowhere. John and I had muddy, nasty pants on and were beginning to wonder if we would be able to get back on track. As we trudged on through the swamp it eventually got dry again and we were looking at about a mile or two of trees and

74

dead leaves. We finally saw a gravel road and started to proceed down the windy path. It soon led us to the lakefront where we could see across to the seemingly tiny campground where John and I were staying. Civilization seemed so close yet so far away at the same time.

We proceeded on foot down the gravel road, which led to a radio tower. But wouldn't you know it, ANOTHER DEAD END!!! So we had to go back into the woods and hope for the best. On and on we went, making stops for water occasionally, but it went on for hours, at least in my mind. Suddenly emerging over a hilltop we spotted a truck. The kind driver stopped, allowing us to ask for directions on how to get back to the campground. He told us to follow the road we were on and it would lead us to the highway. So we did as he told us and soon we were on the highway. We traveled solemnly for about twenty or thirty minutes until finally we saw the entrance to the campground.

Although it was a tiring trip, we had fun and still talk about it. Over all it took almost five hours from when we started on the trail to when we got back, but it seemed like it took the whole day. God helped us find our way back home.

A Truce – by Adam

"Science without religion is lame; religion without science is blind."
- Albert Einstein

The Strege Clan: Grandpa (and Grandma), 6 kids with spouses, and 18 grandkids. There are enough of us that it's hard to apply a cover-all label. But there are two truths that apply to many of us: we are people of God, and we are people of science. Among devout believers and clergymen, there are numerous engineers and those with an innate curiosity in our physical world. Here in 2009 two more cousins enter university for engineering studies, even as Grandpa, my parents and many other family members carry on their unending, important mission in God's name.

Though our tight-knit family gets on well, in the greater world there is a clamor rising. The debate pits God versus science. Some researchers claim advances in science challenge the existence of a Creator. In turn, people of faith take many views of science: some readily accept and practice it, while others keep a distance, perhaps ambivalent toward new discoveries. Still others flatly reject new claims, however well tested.

Do new findings make belief in God obsolete? Certainly, some discoveries encourage us to take a wider, more flexible view of Creation. Since biblical times, not only have we found that we orbit the sun (not vice versa); we have identified hundreds of planets orbiting suns trillions of miles away, some perhaps with life. But for believers to become defensive about these kinds of facts disservices both religion and science.

Rather, it must be understood that nothing in science necessarily subverts God. In fact, as our knowledge of the universe grows, researchers increasingly remark on how amazingly fine-tuned are the laws and constants of nature. The big bang and the theory of evolution can be appreciated by Creationists once we admit neither undermines Creationism (since much of the Book of Genesis should be accepted as allegory). And disruptive discoveries in fields like quantum physics remind us just how little we truly know about our mysterious universe.

Why do we believe? The question is as old as belief itself, and for adults the answer must come after deep introspection. Some have profound gratitude for life and experience; they find this universe too grand to simply "be". Others find life's vicissitudes too hard to bear without reliance on God. And all humanity looks to religion's vast canon (notably the Bible) for moral and legal guidance.

Belief is not about physical facts; as yet there are no provable equations at our disposal. Belief is an element in our wider worldview, a part of the lens through which we make sense of our lives. It does not conflict with science; rather, the two comprise the "Non-Overlapping Magisteria" of the great evolutionary biologist Stephen Jay Gould. Science brings us profound awareness while easing suffering for humankind, and its role will continue to grow. And God will continue to give hope, unite communities, and encourage us to do good for the purpose of serving a greater cause. They need not clash. After all, if the Streges can get on embracing both God and science, why can't we all?

Power of Prayer – by Leah

I don't remember much about Tanzania. I try to block out whatever I do remember. It was a horrible experience for Eric and me. We had such high hopes about how this experience would change our lives. And, well, it did. Just not in the way we expected.

We had planned on volunteering for three months at an orphanage. Our goal was simple: to help people and to gain some experience working in a developing country. We both wanted to work with non-profits that served African peoples in the future, and we thought this would be a great eye-opener for us and a great way to work our way into that world. But things went horribly wrong, and not in the ways you would expect.

We had expected the lack of amenities – we didn't shower every day anyway, so it wasn't going to be *that* drastic of a change. We had expected a lack of privacy – we had already had our honeymoon. We had expected to have difficulties adjusting – we didn't speak the language and we definitely weren't used to the climate.

But what we weren't expecting was the complete chaos of the situation. The organization, an ironic term considering it had none, with which we were volunteering had no oversight whatsoever. Volunteers did whatever they wanted whenever they wanted. No one went to his or her assignments; people would go on weeklong vacations, just abandoning the responsibilities of their work. This was not what Eric and I had signed up for. We wanted real work, hard work that would really tug at our heartstrings.

The living situation was even worse. Sure, our bathroom was just a room with a seat-less toilet, a bucket of dirty water to try to flush whatever was in the toilet, and a couple of lizards. But we could get over that. It was the other people that made it unbearable. The house was worse than a frat house on Homecoming. People were constantly drinking and smoking, blasting rap music until the middle of the night, partying until they passed out. It was ridiculous. Our room wasn't even attached to the main building and we could make out every word that people were saying because they were so loud. And this was when there were only about fifteen people living there. Over twenty more were expected in the next few weeks.

But still my desire to be there and do some good was stronger than my desire to leave.

It wasn't until I realized something else that I knew we had to get out of there. We had been told that we would be driven to our assignments in the mornings and picked up in the afternoons, a necessary precaution with which Eric and I had reassured ourselves before departing on this trip. But now all of a sudden, I learned that not only did you have to get yourself to your assignment, either by walking or by taking the incredibly dangerous dahlla-dahlla, the only transportation system available in which twenty-plus people jammed themselves into a van made for eight, but also that Eric and I would probably have different assignments, meaning that we would be doing this alone. Arusha wasn't the most dangerous of towns, but it was a big city with a lot of people and the only white people in the entire city lived in our house. We were walking targets for muggings, which happened quite often. Oh, and one of the other volunteers enlightened us that on her first night in Arusha, she saw a man get stabbed and another man attacked with a broken bottle. This was unacceptable for me. And even more unacceptable for Eric. He could not bear the thought of his wife being alone in a huge town in Africa where she didn't speak the language. So we made the decision to leave.

This was an especially difficult decision for me because it made me doubt who I was. Suddenly I was unsure if I could handle the future that I had so thoughtfully prepared for myself. But safety came first and we had no other immediate options.

Once the decision was made, we automatically tried to change our plane tickets. Nothing was available. Not only were we in a situation that made us incredibly uncomfortable, but we were stuck there, and we weren't sure for how long. And it didn't help that on our walk to the airline office, our guide backhanded a four-year-old street child who was just looking for help. That was the last straw. We resolved to try again the next day.

It was hard enough to sleep under a mosquito net in the intense African heat, but our feelings of entrapment made it all the more insufferable. While I tossed and turned, fading into some sort of sleeplike state now and then, I could hear Eric's heart thumping erratically on the bunk below me. I knew that he hadn't slept a wink all night. We had been awake for almost three days, with maybe four hours of sleep here and there. And looking back, we're pretty sure our anti-malarial pills made us a little paranoid. That night was probably the most fearful I've ever been in my entire life, yet there was no immediate danger. There was no one outside the door waiting to hurt me. There was nothing physically wrong with my husband or myself. But the fear that we would be stuck in this unsafe situation for three months was terrifying. Eric stood up and took my face in his hands and asked me if I wanted to pray. I nodded.

The tears rolled down our cheeks as Eric asked the Lord to protect us and bring us safely home. It was one of the most powerful experiences I have ever been a part of. I could feel the Holy Spirit in the room and as the words rolled off of Eric's lips, the tension in the room seemed to ease. Both of our bodies relaxed and I could both feel and hear our hearts gradually slowing. Despite our fears, we felt oddly at peace. The pit of my stomach no longer felt like a battle zone. The frenzied look in Eric's eyes seemed to abate. We were able to calm down and just talk to each other, creating some semblance of normalcy with which to pass the night. We felt reassured that the morning would bring the fate that we were hoping for. This was the first time that I think I truly understood the power of prayer.

Surely enough, the following morning, after some impatient phone calls to the airline office, we learned that one of the standby flights had opened up and we had been booked on a flight to D.C. Our prayer had been answered.

And of course, we had some issues before actually arriving home, like the immigration officials who refused to give us our passports back after they asked us to present them, or the unbelievably heightened security in Ethiopia as a result of all the newly-adopted children on their way to America for the first time, but we eventually made it.

Even though Eric and I had an awful experience full of misadventure and delay, I am incredibly glad that we endured it. Not only did it teach me patience, which is a quality that I rarely possess, but it also realigned mine and Eric's priorities in a way we weren't expecting. I think we're both still in the process of healing from this life-changing experience, healing our hearts and minds from the drastic change this brought upon our futures, but we're better for it now and I think better prepared to face the future together, as one.

Operation Japan – by Drew

After months of having our parents trying to convince us to go on this Japan trip, I decided with work obligations, financial constraints and life insanity in general, I was not going on this trip. At the time of the group's initial Japan trip planning, I was starting the highest profile project of my career as the lead editor for an "observational documentary" series of a famous actress/model. I was dead set against leaving the country for this job. But through the beginning of this process, working with some highly respected directors and producers, I thought there would not be another opportunity to do something like this especially with the job security I had in place. After some thought and discussions with bosses to be gone for a couple weeks, I called Joy, who would become "The Insider." I said, "I'm gonna go to Japan secretly and surprise you guys." She said "Awesome! You should call Chris and see if he would go."

I called Chris. Here is our phone-call:

> Me (to Chris): Dude! I'm gonna go to Japan and surprise the family in Tokyo! You should come too!

> Chris (to me): Sweet! I'm in.

So from there we planned in ultra secretiveness our trip, which would be the craziest, most insane operation I've ever been a part of. Joy would send us the itineraries that the family members were planning on to be at so we could plan accordingly. A Japanese friend of mine here in Los Angeles helped me email and call hotels to speak (in Japanese) for simultaneous bookings to be at the same hotels and dates, but under alias names. The first week would be with the family in Tokyo and Kyoto. The second week of the trip would serve another purpose - to promote my Disc Jockey services in the land of Japan and (figuratively) kick down doors of club owners in my quest for DJ One Shot ® awareness. I handed out about a dozen mix tapes and even more cards to managers at some of the hottest nightclubs, but no Japan response! One thing that was noticeable was most of the tracks playing in the hot spots were about 6 months older than the fresh new track rocking in US club dance floors.

Through this unforgettable whirlwind trip, I had the mindset of producing (& editing once back in LA) a little video/photo presentation to relive it again and again. I have received pictures and videos from everyone that went…I have hours of footage and thousands of photos. I estimate working (organizing/ producing a storyline & editing) on this full time for at least 2 weeks non-stop added up over the period of many months. It is 5 minutes so far, and it probably will not be longer than 10 or 15 minutes MAX…but hope to finish it very soon! With some luck (and many hours of free time), the DVDs will be pressed by the time this book is out! Cheers!

On the loose in Tokyo

Thanksgiving Day KFC – by Joseph

I remember back when I was a young child, probably about 9 or 10, the Strege family would get together for Thanksgiving. One year, we met up at Grandpa's house in the afternoon. The kids sat down at one of the small card tables the parents set up for the kids to eat at outside while the adults all ate inside at Grandpa's table. To avoid all the hassle and time involved with making and cleaning up a Thanksgiving dinner, we had buckets of KFC chicken and mashed potatoes to eat for our elaborate Thanksgiving meal.

After we finished eating, my mom and dad made Zack, Rachel, and I go socialize with the adults even though we begged them to just let us go play in the back yard. After we talked to the adults for awhile, all of the kids snuck out to the back yard and started collecting the fallen leaves and then raked them all down into Grandpa's small garden (A service I still do every fall).

One of the older cousins then decided it would be a good idea for us to turn that pile of leaves into a fort so the parents couldn't find us. All of the cousins spent hours down in Grandpa's garden just building a wall of leaves and sticks that would be able to

82

stand up on its own. I guess the hardworking Strege spirit was ingrained in all of us at a young age. I have no idea how we made the wall of leaves somewhat of a sturdy structure (it was probably the older kids' leadership), but it was extremely cool for me to see us build that fort.

The fort didn't last long as we decided to "test its durability" shortly after we showed it to our parents and to Grandpa. We threw balls at it and then we decided to jump on it and break it. It was reduced to just another pile of leaves rather quickly. All of our hard work was reduced to nothing, but what did we care?

In retrospect, it wasn't so much about building the actual fort as it was about building our relationships with one another. That's a Thanksgiving I will always remember.

Children's Books – by Aaron

A fond childhood memory of grandma and grandpa's house was spending time rummaging through their collection of children's books. Some of my favorites were the Dr. Seuss books. Such classics as *Yertle the Turtle, And to Think That I Saw It on Mulberry Street, If I Ran the Zoo,* and *The Lorax* kept me turning the pages no matter the time of day. These books (along with my parents and grandparents) encouraged reading for pleasure at a very formative age. As a result, my love for reading continues to this day.

This love of reading manifests itself in various ways. I generally read magazines in the morning while eating my daily bowl of oatmeal with peanut butter and brown sugar (try this combination sometime, if you haven't!). As a 4th grade teacher, I thoroughly enjoy reading books aloud to my students, as well. The current student favorite is the Diary of a Wimpy Kid series. And on trips back to St. Louis to my grandparents' house on Lonkar Drive, I am always sure to read at least a few Dr. Seuss stories.

Recently, I have followed in just a couple of the many footsteps my grandfather has led. For several years, my grandpa has read books to the 4- and 5-year-olds at his church. Towards the beginning of this time, when he would tell me how much the children enjoyed him coming in and vice versa, I always thought it sounded like a pretty fun time. Fortunately, I have had a very similar opportunity at my church recently but the kids are even younger, in my case, 2- and 3-year-olds. While the attention spans are short (a few seconds), the conversations sparse and random ("hi!"…ten seconds later…"hi!"), and the bathroom breaks frequent (one every hour) they are an entertaining group of toddlers with whom I have enjoyed reading.

I would like to say thank you to my parents and grandparents for providing me and my two brothers, Andrew and Adam, with an excellent childhood (and life). And thanks for the books and encouragement to read throughout the years. I look forward to doing the same for my own kids someday. But in the meantime I will settle for my twenty-seven 4th graders and twelve toddlers. They keep me busy enough these days!

Cousins – by Zack

One of the most memorable Strege family gatherings was in Galena, Illinois. Two houses were rented for everyone to stay in throughout the gathering. In a previous book Grandpa wrote of the "March of 50's" which occurred at this gathering. Our stay at Galena was one of the few times where everyone from Grandma and Grandpa to the eighteen grandkids was in one place. There was a Golden Tee Golf arcade machine, a hot tub, foosball, and tons of other things to do in each house. My favorite time was when all of the parents went out for dinner and the cousins stayed at the houses. Each younger cousin was paired with an older one that was in charge, I was paired with Chris. It was non-stop fun, at least for the younger cousins, once the parents left. While it was a blast to be with only the seventeen other cousins, I have fond memories of times when adults were there as well.

One night everyone gathered to celebrate Grandma and Grandpa's 50th anniversary. Uncle John wrote a song about the family tree and we all sung it. On the Sunday morning at Galena we even had a mini-church service. I don't remember anything about the service except for the fact that we had one. However, I am sure that if someone walked in with a blindfold they would think an entire congregation was singing. The stay at Galena was a unique occasion, and upon reflection showed me that family gatherings yield lasting memories.

Box of Special Things – by Leah

Anyone who knows me well can tell you that I am not a hoarder. I do not like to hold on to stuff just for the sake of not giving it or throwing it away. I have an insatiable need to de-clutter my life and the lives of those around me. When two of my sisters, one of whom was an avid collector as a child and therefore has like fifty weird collections, and the other of whom has kept every single birthday/Christmas/greeting/sympathy/any other kind of card she has ever received, needed help "going through things," I was there to encourage them to downsize and speed that process along. Needless to say, most of my closest family and friends have been at the receiving end of my insufferable prodding.

Despite my urge to chuck all the non-essentials in my life, however, I am guilty of keeping a small box of sentimental trinkets. My Box of Special Things, pardon the exceedingly cheese-ball name, is filled with a bunch of random stuff that for some reason or another means something to me. Here are just a few of the items inside my ornamented cedar box: an orange, heart-shaped pin that I used to wear in kindergarten because it has my name painted on it; a piece of yellow-green paper with a note written to me by a classmate who committed suicide right after high school; a mood necklace (you know, the ones that change color depending on how hard you push on them) with a cross on it that my best friend gave me in elementary school; a letter written by my sister on loose-leaf paper wishing me a happy 12th birthday and apologizing that she would not be able to make it home for it; a rusty key that I bought for $1 in an antique store as a kid; all the information I have ever received about Lister, the now-6-year-old that I sponsor in Zambia; a book written by a German friend of mine with a very personal inscription.

One other thing in this box is a small, pink waist-apron embroidered with birds, flowers, and my Grandma Strege's name across the top – Vercile. I really have no idea how this apron came to be in my possession, especially since I'm not that much of a baker (though I do make a mean oatmeal raisin cookie) and I am really not a fan of the color pink, but this apron is incredibly important to me because not only does it bring to mind all the fun memories that I have of my grandma, but it also reminds me just what kind of a person she was – a servant.

First and foremost, she was a servant of Christ and an excellent example of what that is to those around her. She was the most patient woman I've ever met, she was kind, she was gentle, and she exuded love.

Secondly, and this is where most of my memories kick in, she was always more concerned about other people's needs than her own. In almost all of my memories of my grandma, she was doing something for someone else. When we would sit down to eat a meal, despite our protests, she would make sure that everyone had everything he or she needed before sitting down herself. We kids would usually be almost done by the time she sat down. And then she would clean up the table while Grandpa trekked down to the basement to bring up dessert – cookies and ice cream. Oh, the cold chocolaty goodness of her frozen chocolate chip cookies. I was always so amazed that a frozen cookie could be soft. It was magic!

One of the best times I've had in my entire life was making cookies with her one time. I don't know why, but for some reason it was just me and her – not one of my three sisters was around, which practically never happened in my childhood (maybe that's why it was so special!). I remember her standing beside me and helping me wield the giant cookie dough gun as I tried to force the lion and the rhino through the stencil and out the end of the gun. I don't think we were baking for any special occasion, just for fun, and I just remember being so excited to be helping my grandma with something. I felt important I guess. That's it – Grandma made you feel important.

And then she was always waking up early to make us pancakes when we'd visit. She would make them shaped like Mickey and then Grandpa would bring them to life with expressions made of butter. And she would make sure to give me a metal tumbler because she knew I liked the way it made my milk super cold.

And she would make special trips to the bakery to get us Gooey Butter Cake. And she and Grandpa would read *Go, Dog, Go* to me over and over, even though it's really not the best book in the world. Even after I threw up on the inside of her car one time (I had a bad migraine and had eaten macaroni & cheese and I couldn't help it!), she was more concerned that I get to sleep than about the state of her car (did I mention she was a patient woman?).

Basically, Grandma was the best.

Strege Grandchildren (from left) in 1996 -- Seth, Luke, Ashley, Tara, Leah, Hayley, Joy, Chris, Joshua, Benjamin, Matthew, Adam, Andrew, Rachel, Aaron, Zack, Joseph Not pictured -- Faith.

Strege Grandchildren in 2005 — Sitting: Ashley, Zack, Rachel, Luke, Matthew, Benjamin, Joseph. Standing: Faith, Hayley, Leah, Andrew, Aaron, Joy, Seth, Joshua. Not pictured — Tara, Chris, Adam.

Part 3 Long Ago

The "Long Ago" part of the book title, "How Long is Long Ago?" points to things of the past. This section picks up on that "past" of the Paul and Vercile Strege family as background that made the happenings of Parts 1 and 2 possible.

Ludell, Kansas, 1920

It was less than two years after the Armistice was signed ending World War I when my father, Paul Strege, arrived in Ludell, Kansas, to serve as pastor of Immanuel Lutheran Church. But some of the infectious aftermath of WWI, the flu epidemic of 1918, was still plaguing the United States, and the new pastor had hardly arrived in Ludell when he was stricken with the flu. A strange place, strange people, and a strange disease!

But he was graciously taken in by one of the congregation's families in the home of the Henry Holste's. In due time he has nursed back to health, and began a ministry that lasted there in Ludell until his death in 1946.

Meanwhile, since Paul was single and served as both pastor of the congregation and teacher of the parochial school, his parents came from Milwaukee, Wisconsin, to live with and do the housekeeping for him. Relief came in 1922 with the arrival of a young lady, Beata Ruff, to assume teaching duties at the school. In 1923 the pastor and teacher were married, and my father's parents returned to their home in Milwaukee.

In 1924 Paul and Beata had a son, and named him Paul Jr.

One-year old Paul Jr.

What Was It Like?

The wide, open spaces of western Kansas—that's where I was born and spent my childhood. On a clear day you could "see a hundred miles." Well, not really! But we could see a country church steeple from 12 to 15 miles away from "the divide"—a high spot on the slightly rolling hills of the prairies. On occasion we could also see stormy weather clouds or a tornado moving across the prairies. If they approached where we lived it was a signal to head for the cellar, a hollowed out space underground in the back yard with a slightly tilted horizontal cellar door covering the entrance staircase. Only once do I remember evacuating to the cellar, and that time the tornado struck some miles away.

In contrast to the open-air plains outside was the confined space inside the house where we lived. There were two bedrooms upstairs. Each had a small closet, a double bed, a chest of drawers and a chair or two. The two rooms downstairs each had a coal and wood burning stove with stovepipes connected to the single chimney between the rooms. Besides keeping us warm in winter the kitchen "range" provided heat for cooking, baking and heating the only hot water we had. Next to the metal-lined sink with a hand pump was a counter area with cabinets above it for dishes and below it for pots and pans. Above the sink was the only mirror we had in the house since a pan in the sink was the only "wash basin" we had. There was a table and chairs, and behind the stove was the wooden toy box my father had made for us boys.

The Strege Home with Immanuel Lutheran Church at left and School at right background.

The front "living-room," besides a stove in the center, had my father's large desk in one corner, a bookcase along the wall behind the stove and we had a piano along the other wall. A small cot, an easy chair and my father's swivel chair at the desk completed the furnishings. A front window faced a small porch and the street to the west. The front entrance was through the hallway door opening to the front porch

We had an open-air porch attached at the back of the house behind the kitchen. When my brother Art and I became school age it was "enclosed" and roofed over to provide shelter for a summer cot and the family wash machine. -- Toilet needs, of course, were all attended to in the outhouse in the yard behind the living quarters. -- Since the house was not absolutely mouse-proof, we had a few mouse traps handy, but only had to use them once a year or so. The best mouse-bait, of course, was a small chunk of cheese!

Outdoors was a large yard around both sides of the house and at the back there was space for a garden, a small "tool-shed," a barn with garage attached, and a small chicken coop.

Paul celebrates 5th birthday with friend Roy and brother Art

Kitchen Plumbing

It was a bleak winter 1920's day when the accompanying photo of our back porch was taken. In succeeding years the porch was extended over the full width of the house and by the time I was 12 years old even enclosed to accommodate an extra bed for the family, as well as storage area for an electric washing machine and a few other simple conveniences.

Back porch of house where Paul Jr. grew up.

But the underground "plumbing" serving the kitchen sink was already in place at the time of this photo. To the right of the house the pump above the underground cistern is visible. The cistern with concrete lining held what I would estimate as many hundred gallons of clean water filled in periodically through a rubber hose from the well about 60 feet behind the house and 60 feet deep. Above the well was a long-handled pump used daily to bring water by the bucketful into the house as drinking water. When the cistern needed filling a small gasoline engine and pulley arrangement assisted in pumping the water through the hose to the cistern. An underground pipe from the cistern was connected to a small hand pump at the kitchen sink for pumping water into a water basin for washing face, hands and dishes, as well as shaving, shampooing and similar purposes. We did not drink that water since it was stale and possibly slightly polluted. If hot water was needed it had to be heated in a teakettle on the

94

kitchen stove. – So there were two "grades" of water available in the kitchen—fresh water for drinking with a ladle in a bucket, and water pumped out of the cistern for washing purposes.

Behind the house a concrete top covered the cistern with a covered manhole so that when necessary to clean it, a person could be lowered into the cistern once a year or so. Also an outdoor pump was built into the concrete above the cistern, visible on the photo as a metal box about four feet high. The handle outside the pump was connected to a wheel inside the box geared to a set of chains linked to a series of cup-like containers hanging down into the cistern. When the handle was turned it raised the containers filled with water, and as they rolled over the wheel at the top, poured the water into a spout extending outside the pump into a bucket or other container for use in the yard. -- The principle in play was sort of the reverse of the old waterwheels above a stream which were turned by the water flowing into their "cups," buckets or paddles on the wheel to grind grain in the mill.

There was another underground cavity in the back yard that served as a cesspool into which the water from the kitchen sink drained through a pipe. The cesspool was not fully lined in concrete since the purpose was to let water seep into the soil in the back yard. It was located approximately where the cameraman who took the backyard photo was standing. The cover of the cesspool was hidden under a layer of soil, and we were warned not to allow much weight above the cesspool so the top would not collapse into the cavity beneath. A small pipe extended up into the yard to release foul air from the cesspool and to indicate the area of the yard where we usually did not play.

Home Delivery

No, not of the mail, but of babies! Home deliveries were "in" in the 1920's. Babies were not born in hospitals, but doctors came to the home when a birth took place. At least that was true in Ludell, Kansas and Farrar, Missouri. Paul Strege, Jr., was born in the second-floor bedroom of the Immanuel church parsonage in Ludell in 1924. His wife, Vercile Schmidt, was born in the home of her grandparents Lorenz, with whom her widowed mother was living in Farrar, in 1927.

Paul's birthplace in Ludell, KS.

Vercile's birthplace in Farrar, MO.

The Farrar Lorenz home was one of about a dozen village homes along a hillside road. A church and school were located on the upper end of the road. At the bottom of the hill was the Farrar

General Store where both foods and general merchandise were sold. At the time the accompanying photo was taken the building also housed the Farrar Post Office, and was managed by one of Vercile's cousins, Earl Lorenz.

Farrar General Store, 1992.

Autos Go Modern

By 1922 the price of a mass produced Model T Ford had gone down to $295. By 1925 a new Model T was emerging from the assembly lines every 15 seconds, and by spring 1927 Ford had produced its 15,000,000[th] car. During those boom years other manufacturers were also producing cars, and when I was born in 1924 the competitors were beginning to look more modern, as the accompanying photos of "Baby Paul" may indicate.

Where or when he bought it I don't know, but when I was a baby my father drove a Willys-Overland automobile. The cabin was enclosed with isinglass-like windows in black "flappy curtains" to keep out the weather. In 1928—when I was four—he traded it in for a new 4-door all-steel-enclosed-body Chevrolet with glass windows that could be rolled up and down.

Infant Paul on a summer day at hood of new car.

Babe in arms is Paul Jr.

I don't remember the Willys but very vaguely recall the trip to Kearney, Nebraska, where the Strege family upgraded to the 1928 Chevrolet. There were still numerous Ford Model T cars and trucks around Ludell when I was small, but they gave way to the Ford Model A and many other models. It was the 1928 Chevy that I learned to drive at age 12. (see "How Small is Small?" p.24)

Really modern 1941 Chevy!

Backyard Pool

As popular as they've become in the last few decades in suburban America, backyard pools are not as new as they might seem. -- Proof? The accompanying photo of a 1920's style backyard pool! I enjoyed it over 80 years ago!

Paul Jr. in backyard tub.   Helping with the gardening.

Another backyard activity was gardening, and from little on up Paul Jr. and his brother, Art, were encouraged to help their father.

Oh, yes, and also went to church with parents, this time all dressed up as guests at a wedding.

My father should have found a better place to hide his hat!

A Bird for the Ages

The well-mowed weeds in the Ludell yard on one side of our house almost looked "grassy," and became the locale for numerous family pictures. Since there was not much rain there was no need of "props" besides the occasional blanket on the "lawn." And on this sunny day for the picture of "Mother Strege" and my little sister, Ruth, a friendly bird on the fence has been preserved as "a bird for the ages," printed here 78 years later.

100

Bird for the ages on fence.   Sister Ruth.

The Woodpile

My father's salary during the depression years in the 1930's-- $70, reduced by 10% to $63 a month during the worst years— was supplemented by food and fuel which congregation members delivered to the parsonage as available. The fuel consisted of wooden log segments hauled to the backyard by horse-drawn wagon.   Some of the younger men of the congregation would then come by and split the sawn logs into smaller pieces, which would fit into our kitchen range and living room stove. As brother Art and I grew older we learned to split the logs ourselves, handling an axe well enough to get the job done, even if it wasn't "professional."

A sad saga with the woodpile happened when one of our pet cats was climbing around on it and a log slipped, fell on the cat's leg and broke it. As I recall, the cat must have gone off somewhere to die alone, and we didn't have to arrange a "funeral."

Choo Choo Train

Of course, it was a choo-choo train! There weren't any other kind in those days! And as the photo shows, the toys were made almost "life size" for a small boy! It wasn't too many years later that I also received a steel airplane—Charles Lindbergh style—that was so big we didn't have any other place in our small house to store it except under the bed.

Paul Jr. with a favorite toy

Not all toys were that large, though. And as you might remember from seeing them in museums, some of them were cast iron—a coupe style car (the rumble seat could be opened and closed), a kitchen range modeled after a real one, and whatever else! Apparently we gave them all away when my mother broke up housekeeping after my father died.

Another favorite among them was a steel "steam shovel," about the size of the choo-choo train. It had a swivel top section with a movable scoop. There were two handles to operate it with right and left hands, and it really worked without batteries or switches or electrified motors. Where I loved to play with it was in the ditches along the road behind the school and barn in our neighborhood. The inner edges of the ditch worked well to "build roads" for our little cars "along the side of the mountain," and the steam shovel was a realistic tool to accomplish it all.

Ah, childhood! Sure, our hands got dirty, as did our overalls, but Mom never seemed to complain as long as we washed the hands before we ate—and the overalls went into the weekly laundry with the rest of the clothing!

Downtown Ludell

The "downtown" business section of Ludell (population 100) was two blocks south of our home. Along the street to the left stood the post-office, a hardware store, a general grocery store and the bank. In the next block was the Foster Lumber Company (until it burned down during my childhood) another grocery store, the pool hall/saloon, auto-repair and blacksmith shops, and a gasoline "filling station." The railroad station was a half-mile farther to the south, served by a daily passenger and mail service train. The streets were not paved, so were dusty during dry weather and muddy when it rained.

1918: Stores in downtown Ludell (six years before Paul was born). [Photo credit: Diary of Louise von Engeln Holthus 1907-1925]

1992: Only corner bank and one store remain.

Our daily family routine was a walk to the post-office to pick up the mail from our lockbox #23 and stop in at any other store for shopping needs.

Life was simple, unsophisticated and usually congenial.

School

A one-room school—Immanuel Lutheran—served the educational needs of Lutheran children in and near Ludell. There were up to 40 pupils in 8 grades. Almost all the pupils walked to

104

school even from two and more miles, and brought their lunch bags along. On bad-weather days children of a family almost three miles from school would come in a horse-drawn buggy and tether the horse in the barn behind the parsonage during the day.

One room schoolhouse, teacher Beata in foreground.

Brother Art is third from the left (front row). Paul Jr. is third face from right (just behind front row).

High School Freshman Art and Senior Paul in their band uniforms.

Growing Up in St. Louis

While I was growing up in Kansas, Vercile Schmidt was growing up in Missouri. Her father died before she was born in Farrar. Some years later, her mother married a widower uncle of Vercile's, Eldor Petzold, who had a son, Ralph. They moved to St. Louis and in due time baby Melba joined the family.

The three children attended the parochial school of St. John's Lutheran Church, the church in which Vercile and I were married in 1948.

Vercile and Ralph.   **Vercile and Melba.**

Lutheran Church practice includes Biblical instruction in the upper grades of elementary school for the rite of Confirmation, usually administered in the eighth grade. Considered a special milestone in physical and spiritual growth, parents usually arranged for professional studio photos of the confirmands. This happened in Kansas for me in 1938 and for Vercile in St. Louis in 1941.

Confirmation photos of Vercile (1941) and Paul (1938).

Country Boy Soliloquy

There is a saying that reads: "You can take a boy out of the country, but you can't take the country out of the boy." Reflecting on a lifetime, I tend to feel that the saying is true.

The "country" I come from is not a rural farm, but a small town surrounded by rural farms. I grew up during "depression days" in the 1930's and 40's in a town of 100 people—more or less—in western Kansas. There was only one church in town, and a majority—but not all—of the residents were members of the church or its "mother church," four miles away.

Everybody knew everybody else, if not intimately, at least by face and name. And there was a common concern for each other's welfare, although that was apparently more visible among the "church people," than among them and the "town people." So if someone was ill or in need, there was a readiness in most cases to be of help—by sharing a meal or a few hours of care.

At the same time, there was also a tendency to gossip. Since "everybody knew everybody else," there also tended to be a readiness to listen to and believe whatever people reported about their neighbors. There were even a few "busybodies," persons who seemed to "know everything about everybody," and did not hesitate to pass it on.

The pastor of the church in town (my father) and his family were the beneficiaries of positive concern of most of the people of the town—from congregation members who shared various food items when his salary did not meet the needs (one family delivered milk to the parsonage every day} to the owner of the a local grocery who permitted us to "charge" costs for items purchased that ran up to multiples of the pastor's monthly salary which fell in arrears to similar amounts until bumper wheat crops beginning in 1939 "broke the depression" and all bills were paid up and balances cleared.

There was mutual respect among residents and there was a feeling of contentment despite difficulties, which we children carried into adulthood. We recognized and appreciated it as differing from city or urban attitudes which were conceived of as being more self-centered and resulted in "me-first-ness," and even cheating, mistrust of others and in some cases, crime.

When this "country boy" was literally "taken out of the country" (the U.S.A.), into another country and culture as a missionary to Japan, I felt the transition was relatively easy, and thank God for the experience of being able to carry a "country boy" attitude into the new setting, even when living in Tokyo, one of the largest cities of the world.

"Country boy" Paul and interpreter, Mrs. Arai, with city high school students at first Christmas celebration in Asahigawa, Japan, 1949

Memories of Grandparents

"I turned around so fast that I saw my back!" That was Grandpa Ruff at his best! He always tried to do something to make us— his grandsons—laugh. Actually, my brother, Art, and I never saw our grandparents very often because we lived hundreds of miles from either set of them. We grew up in the depression 30's, which limited travel by car, train or bus.

So when we did manage to travel the 200 miles to Boulder, Colorado, grandpa—a retired Lutheran pastor—made it a point to entertain us with jokes, or with his "hearing aid." It was before the era of any kind of electronic hearing aids, so he had a sort of inverted "bullhorn" with its small mouthpiece end flaring out to amplify the voice when trying to speak to large crowds in those days. Only this "inverted" model's small end fit into the ear with the large flared intake end meant to gather the sound waves coming toward it and magnify the sound as it entered the ear.

We never got to know our grandmother Ruff at all because she died when we were very young. Grandpa remarried and the

110

"grandma" we knew as Carrie, never really related to us except to prepare the meals during our visits. Occasionally they would address each other with "Oh, Papa!" or "Oh, Carrie!" I never could figure out whether they were expressions of endearment or reprimand. – My last visit with them on our way to Japan in 1949 is reported in "How Small is Small?" p. 50.

The Strege grandparents were even less a part of our lives since we traveled to Milwaukee only when I was very young, and I remember them more from photos than in person. But my grandfather Strege was in good health until old age and reportedly went to church at age 96 the Sunday before he died.

Reflecting on the lives of the grandparents includes thanks to God for their commitment to and sharing of their Christian faith with their families, even to my generation.

Grandpa Ruff 1922, Paul & Art with Grandpa and Grandma Strege 1932

Generational Wedding Photos

Paul Strege & Vercile Schmidt – 1948

Paul Strege Sr. & Beata Ruff – 1923

Heinrich Strege Sr. & Louise Gaedtke – married in 1876

Family Portraits

Heinrich Strege Sr. Family – Emma, Frank, Helen, Martha (back row), Louise, Paul, Henry Jr., Heinrich (front row) in 1896.

John F. Ruff Family – Twins Beata & Emma, John Ruff, Gertrude, Martin, and Helena in 1906.

Paul Strege Sr. Confirmation, 1905

Beata and Emma Ruff Confirmation, 1908

EPILOGUE

What to do with someone who lives too long?

In my case—following a practice of giving recognition to clergy celebrating ordination anniversaries in 5-year increments—the Central States Synod of the Evangelical Lutheran Church in America answered that question by preparing a framed 60th Anniversary certificate of recognition for me. Since I was not present to receive it at the biennial Synod Assembly in Kansas in June, long time friend Bishop Gerald (Jerry) Mansholt arranged for presenting it to me at a special church service in our St. Louis congregation on Sept. 6, 2009.

It turned out to be more of an event than I deserved. As a surprise, five of my six children and their spouses, plus a number of grandchildren and a great-grandson were present to greet me (one family couldn't make it because of a wedding in Cleveland). My brother and two of his children and families were also among the worshippers. I was ushered to a front row seat and the celebration began with a lusty hymn by the congregation, whose members filled the sanctuary.

The Bishop preached a masterful sermon around the Scripture readings for the day on a theme entitled "How God is God!" apparently patterned on the style of my book titles (e.g., "How Small is Small?"), but with an "exclamation mark" instead of a "question mark." He made reference to a number of experiences in my life from the place of my birth to my 85th birthday, all of which he must have researched extensively. My two "musical" sons put together a medley of my favorite hymns for piano and violin (John on piano, Mark on violin) — so impressive that several congregation members requested later that it be used at their funerals.

At the end of the worship, formal citations from the Synod, International Partners in Mission, the Governor of Missouri, and a local representative in the Missouri legislature were presented, the latter two through the efforts of Perry Nelson, music director of St. Thomas/Holy Spirit Lutheran Church.

To God be the glory!